FORBIDDEN LAND

A Saga of Tibet

By the same author

WHEN IRON GATES YIELD

GOD HOLDS THE KEY

THE SKY IS RED

CORAL IN THE SAND

FORBIDDEN LAND

A Saga of Tibet

By
GEOFFREY T. BULL

MOODY PRESS
CHICAGO

First printed 1966

Published by special arrangement with
HODDER AND STOUGHTON, LONDON

Moody Press Edition 1967

Printed in the United States of America

CONTENTS

To my three sons, Ross, Peter and
Alister, who asked for a story; and to
all the young people of their generation,
this book of pioneer trekking in the
great wild-west of the Sino-Tibetan
borderlands, is written.
It is sent out in the hope that in
this age when drift and futility sap the
life-blood of youth, many may find
that to follow Christ where He leads,
is still the greatest adventure of all.

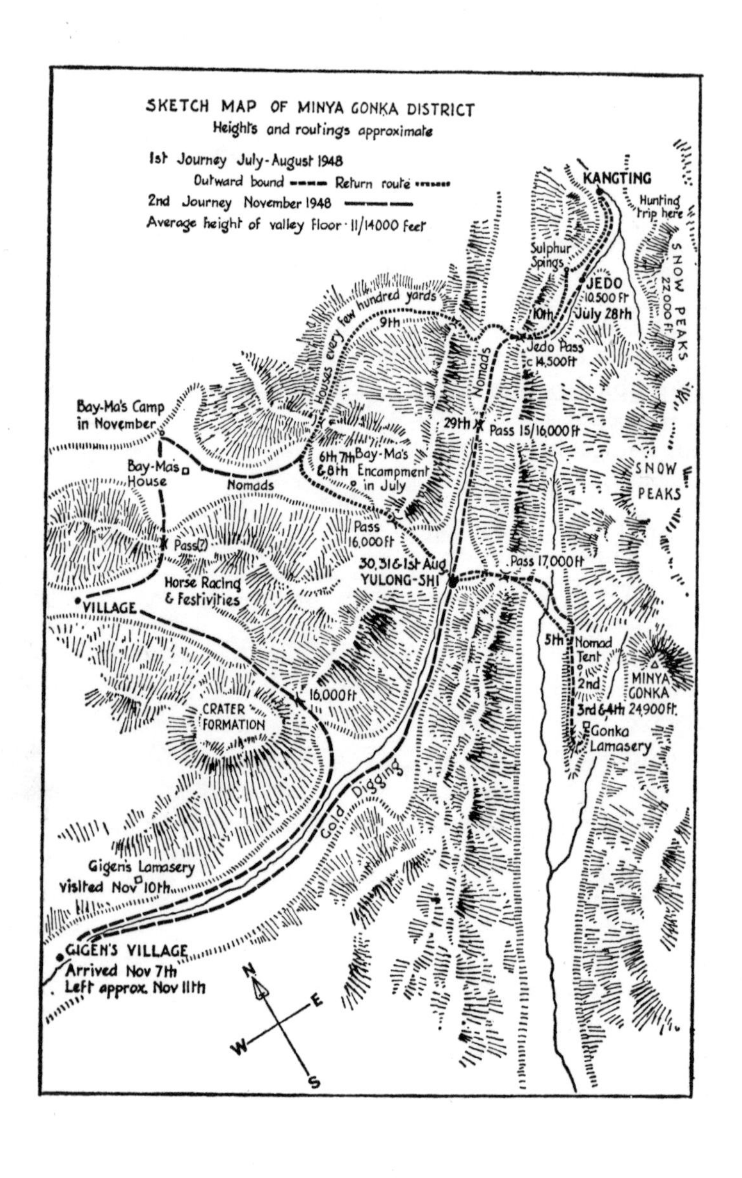

SKETCH MAP OF MINYA GONKA DISTRICT
Heights and routings approximate
1st Journey July-August 1948
Outward bound Return route
2nd Journey November 1948
Average height of valley floor · 11/14000 feet
KANGTING
Hunting trip here
Sulphur Spings
JEDO
10,500 Ft
July 28th
10th
SNOW PEAKS
22,000 Ft
Houses every few hundred yards
9th
Nomads
Jedo Pass
c 14,500 Ft
Bay-Ma's Camp in November
29th
Pass 15/16,000 Ft
6th 7th & 8th
Bay-Ma's Encampment in July
SNOW PEAKS
Bay-Ma's House
Nomads
Pass 16,000 Ft
Pass(?)
30, 31 & 1st Aug
YULONG-SHI
Pass 17,000 Ft
Horse Racing & Festivities
VILLAGE
5th
Nomad Tent
2nd
MINYA GONKA
24,900 Ft.
3rd & 4th
16,000 Ft
CRATER FORMATION
Gonka Lamasery
Gold Digging
Gigen's Lamasery
Visited Nov 10th
GIGEN'S VILLAGE
Arrived Nov 7th
Left approx. Nov 11th
N
E
W
S

CHAPTER ONE

THE TALE OF A TAIL

WE made a great start. The sky was blue, the peaks above a shimmer of snow, and the sunshine an irrepressible sparkle in the pure mountain air. Down through the rocky defile our horses carefully picked their way but we ourselves hardly thought about the trail, for our eyes were intoxicated with the sheer grandeur of the scene. We took lunch at a ramshackle inn which, contrary to expectations, produced some very good fried rice, then pressed on towards Luting. The road became sandy and the horses thirsty. Grotesque cactus formations marked the way and we looked in vain for any vestige of pasture. In the valley below, the wide, swirling waters of the Tung-Ho moved silently and swiftly out from the vast Central Asian plateau, and onwards to the quiet paddy-country of the Szechwan plains. Riding at a slow, jogging pace our eyes were drawn irresistibly towards its mesmerising flow. The hours passed and soon the afternoon sun was dipping over the ridges. As darkness fell, the track narrowed, and we found ourselves groping along a meagre shelf of rock some six feet wide. On our right the harsh face of the hillside rose abruptly into the unknown, while to our left the cliffs dropped away to the murky depths of the river, flowing on relentlessly into the night. Head to tail, our horses nosed their way along, with Loshay in the lead and with George and myself bringing up the rear. It was pitch black now and no one spoke. Only the crunch of rock under hoof broke the stillness of our crisis. The minutes seemed to us like hours. Then suddenly we turned around a spur of rock to glimpse the twinkling lights of human habitation. It was the Chinese town across the river.

As we reached the wire-rope bridge, strung precariously some fifty feet above the water, we were confronted with an even more terrifying dilemma. This tenuous mode of communication, stretching some hundred yards out there into the darkness, was as tremulous as a spider's web. Dare we take the horses over? Would they panic as the slender rope-work swayed? The alternative was to spend the night in the open, but after twelve hours on the road we could hardly face that either. There was a pause for quiet deliberation. Then we decided to venture. George went first, as his horse was undoubtedly our most sensitive animal. Feeling for every foothold on the ragged wooden slats, he slowly disappeared down the foot-walk, swallowed up in the darkness. If ever his prayer approached 'vain repetition', George said it was then. Loshay, our Tibetan boy and an intrepid nomad from the grasslands, followed. He had our 'cheapest horse', an animal, let it be said, more or less 'non-sensitive', and just a plodder. We called her 'the Gebo' which means in Tibetan, 'the Aged One'. About ten yards out over the river 'the Gebo' plunged downwards. It was a sickening moment. Doing her best as she always did, the worst had overtaken her. She had plodded right through a gap in the boards. At first there was such bedlam, what with Loshay shouting and the horse's hooves scrabbling, that I could hardly tell what had happened, but a local youngster, attracted to the scene and carrying a tiny oil lamp, came to our assistance. By the light of this diminutive flame, I moved out gingerly to survey the situation. It was an appalling predicament. The Gebo lay with her stomach astride three wooden boards and her four legs dangling into space. Between brief 'breath-getting' periods, the poor Gebo fought to raise herself. With frantic and convulsive movements she strove for a hoof-hold but all to no avail. At every lunge the whole bridge rocked alarmingly. One false step and we would go spinning headlong into the abyss, to have our bodies swept downstream to the Pacific nearly two thousand miles away. And what was more, if the lad with the lamp fell to his death, the whole town would rise up and stone us. To pronounce the Gebo a 'night-*mare*', in any other situation might pass as a pun but things were already beyond humour. It would only need another horse to falter and we would be stranded the whole night on the bridge. We were juggling with life and death on a tight-rope. What could we do? As the foot-walk was little more than three feet wide it was impossible to turn back. George was obliged to go forward and I needed to stay where I was. At this juncture Loshay's built-in Tibetan calm began to assert itself. He now took charge. The first thing was to unsaddle the Gebo. How the equipage did not dive into the depths below remains a mystery, but once relieved of all encumbrances the Gebo renewed her struggles. She was pathetic in the extreme. Loshay heaved desperately at her bridle. The wooden slats skated hither and thither. She almost succeeded in rising, but not quite. Grabbing her tail I exerted all my strength to give the final lift she needed. In my anxiety however, I had forgotten what tails were made of! The long, hairy, but basically solid appendage arched frighteningly, until it stood a full right-angle to the creature's spine. Loshay took one horrified glance at what I was doing and howled, "Mi nyan! Mi nyan!"—"No good! No good!" One more degree, I guess, and the tail would have snapped from its base! Grunting and gasping the Gebo at last responded to this drastic leverage and stood triumphantly, albeit tremblingly, on her four feet again. Whilst I stood by the loads and saddle bags, Loshay now led the horses one by one to the farther side. That God was with us, we could not doubt, for the boy made the hazardous journey of some eighty yards in complete darkness, no less than four times. Not one horse fell through the boards again and neither did we! I could not help thinking in the circumstances of Luke's description of the shipwreck and how his fellow-passengers reached the beach in safety. 'And so,' he says, 'it came to pass, the rest, some on *boards* . . . escaped all safe to land.'

This incident provides us with a Tibetan 'tale' in more senses than one, but before we trek together through the great Tibetan uplands, visit the nomads in their tents, tread the shadowed courts of the lamaseries, and even risk the brigands' guns, I would like to tell you just how George and I came to be with Loshay in such a remote part of the world.

CHAPTER TWO

SIGNPOST TO TIBET

As a teenager one of the gnawing questions at my heart was 'Why am I here?' Coupled with this were the comparable enigmas, 'Where have I come from?' and 'Where am I going?' Unless I could gain a clear answer to such enquiries, then all my life was a question-mark and I did not want it that way. I longed for life to be positive and vital, enthusiastic and real; in fact, an exclamation-mark right the way through! Did God just toss His stars into the sky, scatter daisies in the meadows and give His babies to anyone? Was the universe one vast happy-go-lucky affair, capricious, meaningless and devoid of lasting worth and values? On investigation, it did not really appear so. As a human being I generally meant what I said and did what I intended. Could God be less in His will and purpose than I His creature? If God's actions were intentional then they *were* meaningful. That I had life, was an act of God. My parents were not its source. They merely transmitted it. If all God's actions had meaning, then the key to life must be in God Himself. When quite a youngster I professed to trust in Christ. What that profession meant I cannot possibly now assess, but I know there came a time when the Lord Jesus became a living reality to me. Once He did then I knew He had a purpose for me, because Christ is God come down to earth to bring us His plan. This plan makes it possible for a man to enter God's family and to know His fellowship so that life becomes a doing with Him, those things which He Himself, has planned that I should do. In other words, a fulfilling of my destiny; doing that for which I was born; realising the purpose for which Christ redeemed me. Then it is that all the answers begin to shine. Then I can say, I have come from the hand of God. I am here for the sake of God; and one day I am going to be with God. If we do not know this, then we are lost in every sense of the word. 'But how do you find out what God wants you to do?' someone will ask.

Now let me be perfectly frank. Up till my last term at school everything was a frightful bore. If I played football, then we were sure to lose and I would be dropped from the team. If I played cricket, I would be dismissed for some uncertain reason like L.B.W., a verdict which was always aggravating for, after all, the ball might never have hit the wicket. Games therefore were only a disappointment. I always seemed to be the odd man out. When it came to lessons there was of course, that bugbear Chemistry, with 'Fireworks' the science master, to contend with every time. And what more explosive name than Bull could you find for a launching pad. It really was most disheartening. As for French—this, for me, was the most miserable language in the world. Chinese and Tibetan were as nothing compared to this hurdle of my schoolboy years. In Chinese you do not spell. In Tibetan the spelling is completely regular, but in French there is not a word that sounds like it looks. By the time I got to that last year I was just 'fed up' with it all. To make matters worse I failed 'the matric' the first time and that meant, in those days, I had to take a fresh selection of set-books the next year. 'Macbeth' I could tolerate, what with its witches, its blood and thunder and even a sleepwalk, but 'A Midsummer Night's Dream' and 'The Rape of the Lock'—I felt these 'monstrosities' were just so much nonsense foisted on the minds of innocent and sensible teenagers before they had a chance to leave school and make a run for it! But one day in the Easter holidays, just a few months before I left school, everything was changed. My negative, resentful outlook was broken to pieces. I had a fresh encounter with God.

It all happened in a most unexpected way. Having nothing to do in the holidays, I attended a series of outings, games and meetings arranged by one of the local evangelical churches. In some way or other, I allowed myself to become involved in a young people's prayer-meeting. Normally speaking I would have kept clear of anything like this but there it was, I was in it now and had to sit it through. Then suddenly, to my blank astonishment, the leader announced "We are *all* going to pray". This was not a formal intimation of the commencement of a meeting. He really meant it, and pointing to the youngster at the end of the row he said in a matter-of-fact way, "Now we'll begin with you!" To my utter amazement the young person stood up at once and without demur prayed simply and sincerely with no apparent effort or nervousness. Then the next young person stood and then the next. I was dumbfounded. The panic in my heart reduced me to such a state that I would have trembled all over had I not been so busy tensing myself for the awful moment. How could I ever do it? Yet how could I not do it? Hardly knowing what I did I rose stoically to my feet.

'It' had come to me. I have not the faintest recollection of what I said but I did say something and then sat down. It had been a humiliating experience, yet once it was over an unexpected joy began rising within me. I could not account for this at first, but the fact was that the hidden faith in my heart had been forced out into the open. I had feared to pray openly just as I had feared to speak of Christ openly. Although I had been shamed into this public act of prayer yet notwithstanding I had made my confession and now I just longed to tell people about Jesus. We may believe in our hearts, but it is confessing with our mouth Jesus as Lord that brings us into the assurance and joy of our salvation. The days that followed were very wonderful to me. The Light of Life, of which Jesus spoke, was shining in my soul.

One night I arrived late at a meeting and because the speaker had commenced his talk I felt I could not go in. It was a cold night and the snow was falling. I stood waiting on the steps wondering what to do. Then I was joined by another late-comer, a young fellow about my own age. We chatted together and I soon discovered he did not know Christ as his Saviour. As the meeting proceeded inside, so outside on the step I told him what it meant to be saved. I spoke of the wonder of knowing 'The Son of God loved me and gave Himself for me'; to realise, 'It is no longer I but Christ liveth in me'; to be able to face God with every sense of guilt removed and to walk with Him and work with Him; to be in the Divine Plan; to know that life is not futile but brimming with his purpose. He listened intently, and as the time went by I ventured to ask of him, "You realise you *can* be saved, don't you?" "Yes," he said . . . "Well, do you *want* to be saved?" I continued. "I do," he replied. Finally I put the question, "Are you *willing* to be saved?" To my great joy he answered, "I am willing", and there, as we sheltered from the snow, we bowed our heads and he received Christ into his heart. Looking back now, I feel this was the very first soul I ever led to the feet of my Lord. In bringing His good news to others the purpose of God was unfolding before my eyes. It is when we personally submit to Him that we begin to have an experience of His guidance. We may be only lambs in His flock, but if we keep close to the Shepherd we shall not fail to hear His voice, and soon He will give us things to do.

Now the time came when God was to show me in greater detail His plan for my life. After leaving school I eventually went to work in a bank. Each morning before I left for the office I would read a portion from my old Bible. This particular copy of the Holy Scriptures was bound in red morocco leather and had been given to me on my first birthday. As I grew up and read it for myself it thus became especially mine. One particular morning I was reading in the first chapter of Galatians, when suddenly part of a sentence gripped my attention. The words I read were these, 'Called by His grace to reveal His Son in me'. Adjustment to business life had been hard enough in some ways, bringing its own spiritual hazards. I was still only a junior and could hardly be viewed with less regard than I was by my senior colleagues, yet these words brought me now into a fresh understanding of what it meant to be a Christian. Could it be possible that God Himself should choose a stumbling youth in an office and make him a vessel in which the glories of His own Eternal Son should be displayed? He had done this for Paul, leading him from birth to new birth, flooding his heart with light, then shining through him to the world at large. I began to believe that God really intended to do this for me. The following days found my heart singing at the sense of this vocation. Such was the joy that I decided to return to the same passage and see what further light lay hidden there for me. I found the words I had so gladly embraced were in the middle of a sentence. Eagerly I pursued the sense into the next phrase, which I had completely forgotten. Slowly I read it, 'Called by His grace to reveal His Son in me, *that I might preach Him amongst the heathen*'. The latter words could not be divorced from those which preceded them. Was this also for me? What did it mean? God stilled my heart. He had brought me to this moment. I could only accept the challenge and enter as God might lead into the obedience of His call. So it was I began to believe for the first time in my life that my vocation was to take the Gospel to the nations. My destiny was now revealed. I could never really do what I wanted again.

From that day my life was straightened to His overriding purpose. The war years came, bringing their shadows and perplexities to us all. The call-up started, and young fellows who had been at school with me began to lose their lives in the great conflict that ensued. The Germans reached the channel ports and it seemed impossible that life would ever return to what we always viewed as normal. Missionary work of the kind I envisaged seemed altogether out of the question. Yet 'the things that are impossible with men are possible with God'. In the midst of these great events God spoke to me again showing me very clearly that His call to me must be crystallised in specific service.

At that time it was my custom to keep a little 'prayer-book'. This was a volume of blank pages in which burdens were noted and after a while of intercession the consequent answers written in. This served as a very real stimulus to faith. One page I especially kept for what I called the 'closed lands'. Amongst these were Russia, Brazil, and the Central Asian countries of Tibet and Nepal. One day whilst kneeling in my bed-room, praying for the peoples of these lands, I began to be concerned for the people of Central Asia, and in particular those of Tibet. I knew little of that remote and mysterious country except it was a nation without Christ. The old question from the Scripture came back to me, 'How shall they hear without a preacher?' Yet I could not feel that my personal concern *for them* actually constituted God's personal call *to me*. Never-theless, I was sufficiently moved to pray that if He were leading me to serve Him there, then would He graciously direct me with a specific sign into His perfect Will? I claimed His promise in the Psalms, 'I will guide thee with mine eye', and waited on the Lord to show whether these aspirations were inspired of Him. He was not a disappointment, for 'The Lord worketh for him that waiteth for Him'. Just a short while afterwards I received a letter through the post from a Christian gentleman totally unknown to me. For his part, I was equally unknown to him. He was writing to me, because at that time I was the acting leader of a Bible Class convened in our house. He wondered whether we young men would like to hear something of the missionary work he represented. I opened the envelope and found in my hand the literature of the Central Asian Mission. I saw also that a map of the Indo-Tibetan border had been enclosed, showing points at which the Gospel was already being preached. There was quite a lot of other information about the spiritual needs of Tibet and the surrounding countries. I had never heard of this work before, neither had I been in contact with this organisation. Coming as it did at that very juncture of my life, where through prayer I had been brought into a definite expectation of guidance, I could only accept it as a specific sign that my desire to serve God on the Central Asian plateau was born of Him. Nearly six years elapsed before it was possible for me to go. It was a period of testing and preparation. The war years were a schooling in themselves and provided much opportunity of character training and Christian service. It was in this period that I came in contact with my fellow-worker-to-be, George Patterson of Laurieston. Unbeknown to each other we had both been in contact with a Mr. Harold Avery who was working amongst Tibetans on the Indo-Tibetan border. Sensing our ardent desires towards the people whom he served and feeling that God was calling us to such work, he put George and myself in touch with each other. In 1946, after one or two preliminary meetings, we faced the challenge of Tibet together. We met in George's lodgings in London, where he was taking a course in missionary medicine, and scanned together a large map of the Forbidden Land. With the map lying spread out on the bed we knelt together before God and poured out our hearts to Him concerning His call to go to this darkened people. For hundreds of years the Bhuddist-Lamaistic régime headed by the Dalai Lama had withstood all efforts to bring the Gospel to the Tibetans. Who were we to undertake this task? How could we expect to succeed more than others? But these were not questions that we were required to discuss. God was saying, 'Go in this thy might, have not I sent thee'. Strengthened through our mutual fellowship and prayer, we now sought with all diligence to be ready to leave in the following year. This determination was further fortified by an invitation to go to China which prior to this we had hardly viewed as the door to Central Asia. The way was plainly opening for us and in the Spring of 1947, with the full fellowship of those Christians with whom we worshipped in our own home towns, we set sail for the Far East.

This accounts then for George and I being together on the Chinese-Tibetan border. We were there at God's call to bring the Gospel of Christ to the Tibetans. But where did Loshay come in? Loshay was one of those lovable rascals that abound amongst the young people of the nomad encampments. He first took our eye, riding a mountain pony with accomplished abandon, in a horse race high up in the grassland country where China merges with Tibet. He was only twenty-one then. He had been to Lhasa and back, and was a born rover. True as steel to his friends, he was a terror to his enemies; and as far as the girls were concerned, to say he was 'a rascal' would hardly do him an injustice! He was introduced to us by Bay-Ma. 'And who was Bay-Ma', you may ask? Well, that will bring us to another story.

CHAPTER THREE

OVER TWO-WOLF MOUNTAIN

BEYOND the river Ya the trees and hills lifted eerily into the morning mist. Not a mountain could be seen, but somewhere beyond that mist lay the notorious outback, the land of the world's mightiest ranges, the lair of 'the barbarians'—the unknown, legendary realm of Tibet. Only mention to a Chinese that this was your destination and he would look askance at you, doubting your reason. Prior to the Chinese Communist invasion, few there were that ventured into this hostile hinterland. For them Ya-an* was the last frontier of civilisation beyond which, if you must go, an armed guard was to be preferred. It is not difficult therefore to imagine how I arose with excitement and expectancy, on the morning of departure. Up till now I had travelled on ocean liner, river boat, railway train, 'plane and bus, but as the coolies gathered, shouting and gesticulating over their loads, I was fascinated to see this new form of transport, the mountain chair. It was a distant relative, I suppose, of the old English 'sedan'. It comprised two long poles with a simple hammock of bamboo sticks slung between. A carrier took the weight at either end and a third man ran at the side (that is, if you were *over*-weight!) to act as a relief. I felt it was all rather inhuman and rocked uneasily, both morally and physically, as I was borne along. But this was their rice-bowl and the irony was, of course, that had I

* A town in West China.

chosen to walk, then the carriers would have been the first folk to show their disappointment. Indeed had I known the kind of country through which we were to pass I would have been more thankful for it right from the start. The party with which I was travelling now amounted to quite a caravan. There were thirty-three persons in all. Twenty-five coolies, seven adults of mixed nationalities and a three-month-old 'missionary' baby! There was a total of eleven mountain chairs, but no soldier escort. We were making the journey unarmed; but as trusting the Living God, by no means undefended.

The first day's trek proved the least formidable. The road followed the river for a good distance before we came to the first rope-bridge. This was negotiated a little fearfully by the feminine members of the party but was not really dangerous. Then followed a series of low clay hills which were traversed with comparative ease, the weather being reasonably dry. Even so it was already late afternoon before we dropped down to a small plain and headed for a township called Tien Chuan, some two miles distant. We found there a very good inn by oriental standards. The rooms were dominated by big wooden beams which gave the impression of being below decks on an old sailing vessel but the fact of being some fifteen hundred miles from the sea kept imagination in check. Before retiring the landlord looked in to see us. He was interested to meet the different travellers and to his surprise became suddenly aware of our Unseen Companion. One of the Christians in the party introduced him to Our Lord Jesus Christ.

The next morning it was pouring with rain. The

coolies were militant and, staging a united revolt, declared they would not leave. After much coaxing (coercion is an ugly word) we did eventually persuade them to move. We got rather wet at first, but the weather gradually brightened. The going was rough as we had to pick our way over a low boulder-strewn river bed running down from the hills; but once firmer bridle-paths were reached, the chair-carriers padded along sharply for they were obliged to cover forty miles by nightfall—an incredible distance in the circumstances. As we penetrated further into the mountains the country became more rugged and the valleys deeper. The slopes above us were thickly wooded with conifers and lower down we glimpsed wild rhododendron bursting into bloom. From their fern-enshrouded courses streams cascaded into the open, veiling the dark green foliage with a film-like spray and providing the magnificent spectacle of innumerable waterfalls plunging from the heights into the noisy ravines below. It was exhilarating country giving a foretaste of greater vistas to follow. As the valley narrowed, the trail became the one main route into the plateau. We thus grew more aware of the many tea-carriers along the way. Amongst them there were both men and women, old and young, and even little children, trudging slowly forward in single file with their unbelievable burdens. The maximum weight a man might carry at the peak of his physical endurance would be sixteen bundles of some twenty-five pounds each. That is to say, four hundred pounds—and he would carry it to a height of at least 10,000 feet. This normally impossible feat finds a clue to its explanation in the odd bundle or two carried by the boys and girls. They are gradually tempered to it over the years. It is, of course, a highly hazardous occupation, because the slightest imbalance on the precipitous mountain trails and the load whirls the carrier over the cliff to be pulverised on the rocks hundreds of feet below. It seems that David had watched this happen in the hill country of Judea. 'Mine iniquities', he says, 'are gone over mine head: as a heavy burden they are too heavy for me.' At seven-fifteen in the evening we called a halt at a forlorn collection of tumbledown huts standing at the confluence of the Ya river and one of its tributaries. We were all dog-tired, for the terrain demanded that we walk for long stretches of the stony track. When we saw the accommodation it was as well we were tired. The rooms were black and filthy. The only light was the tiny flame from a length of pith dipped in oil. I shared a room with Gordon, a young missionary who at that time hoped to work with George and myself amongst the Tibetans. We managed to get some sort of meal then bedded down. Ugh! Something unspeakably ghastly was happening! On an unmentionable part of my anatomy a ferocious 'beast' was digging in for the night. In almost panic-stricken haste we reached for the oil lamp then, as Gordon held its flickering flame close in, I wrenched back my clothing. Whatever was it? To look at, it seemed like a small crab! Gordon made one grab at it, and snatched it out of my flesh. I have travelled to many parts of the world since that memorable night but I have never forgotten the monstrous parasites of Liang Lu Kou!

On the third day the country took on even greater dimensions. Each mile was bringing us nearer to the roof of the world. The valley we had been following for the last two days seemed now to drop away and the noise of the rushing water grew softer and more remote as we entered the clouds. We were moving into a strange, silent world of swirling mist and drenching drizzle. We had reached the slopes of Two-Wolf Mountain, the range that marks the great geographical divide between China and Tibet. A long, slow, tortuous climb over mud and rock ensued. The track led us up through the great pine forests and, as always on such occasions, the yearning for the summit began to consume us, forcing our aching limbs to move almost mechanically up the precipitous incline. The three-month-old baby in the party now became the most important bundle of the whole caravan. Each man had a turn at carrying the little one. The altitude taxed our breathing and we all took our own time to reach the top. Then looming out of the mist came an old stone archway. We passed beneath it and to our amazement found we had gained our goal. We were walking 10,000 feet above the level of the sea. The elation of the moment, however, was tinged with sadness. Only an hour from the top, I had made a discovery. The coolies stopped for a breather and some of them disappeared into a hovel nearby. I took a peep inside to see what they were about, and to my sorrow I saw them stretched out on low beds and couches. Beside each man burned a little lamp and in each mouth was a pipe. It was an opium den. Without opium, they said, they could not carry their loads over the passes. I felt condemned, and became persuaded in my mind I could never hire a mountain chair again—and in fact I never did. We now descended a few hundred feet, where we came to quite a sizeable house. The clouds dispersed and we gained our first view of the stupendous territory to the west. We stood indeed on the saddle of a mighty watershed. The appearance of the countryside had changed completely. It was so dramatic that one had the sense of passing from one world into another. From the rain-soaked pine forests we had come, in a few hundred yards, to a dry, treeless landscape of bare-backed ridges extending as far as the eye could see—and somewhere there in the far distance rose the cloud-capped giant of Minya Gonka.

Gordon and I had a good night in this high mountain 'hostelry' called Kan Hai Tzu. Food and drink are simple in these isolated places, but one consolation is that they generally taste better than they look. The standard beverage on Two-Wolf Mountain was bean soup. Served piping hot it went down well. Now came the great descent to the valley of the Tung Ho. On the way down we encountered some of our first Tibetans. What a splendid race they are! When you first see them they stand in marked contrast to the more diminutive Chinese of the Szechwan plains. The Kamba Tibetans are a freedom-loving, debonair mountain people, who can never be tamed. Whether attired in their simple homespun gowns, or their silken robes all edged with beaver and lined with lambskin, it makes no difference. As they pass you, swords and daggers at the ready, and crowned with their jaunty fox-fur headgear, they give you the feeling that they are a band of sixteenth-century buccaneers. Their poise is defiant, but not marred by arrogance. It stems from a pride of race which all down history the Chinese have never once subdued. Boyish at times, they are nevertheless astute judges of character. They are courageous, good-humoured; and, as every tribe in Central Asia knows, born fighters.

Midday saw us in Luting, and by afternoon we had crossed the river by the wire-rope bridge and were skirting its western bank. We trailed along the dusty, sandy route for several hours until at evening time we came to a little hamlet called Pen-Ba. We had been on route four days now and not without reason were beginning to tire. Yet we were by no means the first missionaries to know fatigue along that road. Over the years many attempts had been made to take the Gospel of Christ into this formidable area. As early as 1846 Huc and Gabel traversed it. Cameron also passed this way in 1877, reaching as far as Batang, some three weeks riding to the west. Annie Taylor led her party to the Tibetan border, and little doubt was acquainted with this trail. In 1897 Polhill, one of the Cambridge Seven, opened up Tatsienlu, now called Kangting, to the Gospel. It was this very town we hoped to reach on the morrow. What illustrious names are linked with these spiritual assaults on the devil's bastion of Tibet! There followed men like Meyes, Soutter, Johansen, Amundsen and then Radford, who sought to enter this territory in the early nineteen hundreds shortly after the Boxer rising. Both he and Soutter laid down their lives in the attempt. Men like Sorensen, Edgar, Cunningham, came after them. They may be only names to many but they are men who gave their all to bring the Gospel to the Tibetan people. Now, just a century after Huc and Gabel, we ourselves were arriving to carry forward the torch of the Evangel. Would we be found worthy to follow those who had gone before us? It is no light thing to serve the Lord Christ in the wake of so great a vanguard. We hardly realised it then, but that is what we were doing and we would need all the grace of God to go through to a finish.

The fifth and last day of our journey into the plateau was an unremitting ascent, but it was far from unrewarding, for with every turn of the road we gazed on fresh wonders of towering crags, tumultuous mountain torrents, and distant eternal snows. Gordon and I were like horses straining at the bit, for this was the day when we were to be united with George who, according to plan, had preceded us in the advance to Kangting. There we expected to commence our Tibetan language study and make basic preparations for a further penetration into the plateau a year or so later. It must have been about eleven in the morning when we sighted two figures away up the valley. The chairs and loads were strung out now far down the trail, but nothing could stop us racing forward to be greeted not only by George, whom it was so great to see, but by someone else whom we had come to know and love in China. I refer to John Ting, who in that Satanic stronghold of Kangting had already pointed many to Jesus Christ our Lord.

CHAPTER FOUR

GATEWAY TO THE SILENT GODS

KANGTING, as a city, is one of the most extraordinary places on earth. When we arrived in the spring of 1948 it was the provincial capital of Sikang. At one time powerful Tibetan rule had extended down into China, but over the years the Chinese had gradually forced the Tibetans back into their mountain strongholds, until they had finally annexed some three hundred miles of Tibetan territory. Kangting lay on the eastern extremity of this loosely-governed area, and the result was that it developed into a kind of commercial, and even political clearing house for both the Chinese and the Tibetans. On the streets, two entirely different peoples passed to and fro—different in race, speech, custom, dress and their every demeanour. Notwithstanding their trade transactions still proceeded with some measure of tolerance. The Chinese were generally dressed in rather prim blue gowns which reached to their feet, but alongside them in the shops you might suddenly see a wild-looking nomad from the grasslands. There he would stand, his shock of long, unkempt hair; unwieldy sheepskin gown; and naïve, uncouth manner, drawing uneasy glances from more sedate customers. A huge bare shoulder, bristling with muscular strength and tanned a chocolate brown, would remind them not to make too many adverse comments. With almost childish amusement he would fondle the goods, then with curiosity satisfied, lumber awkwardly into the street. The wry grimaces of the townsfolk meant little to the nomad. Chinese officialdom and the wealthy merchants of the community might look contemptuously upon these 'barbarians' from the hills, but when a big Tibetan trader came riding through the town, dressed to perfection in coloured silk, high-collared shirt and figured boots, they would think again. Sitting astride a well-groomed horse with his servants and well-laden beasts behind him, he would take possession of the road. With such there was no question of inferiority, only a proud return of the Chinese disdain. The tolerance, therefore, was merely superficial and over the months, as Chinese rule began to disintegrate, the Tibetans became more and more intransigent and the atmosphere charged with tension.

The town was the religious headquarters of countless priests known as lamas; and in and out of the homes and monasteries there echoed the dismal Buddhist chant of 'Om! Mani padme hum!' The words mean 'Hail! The Jewel in the Lotus!'—that is to say, 'the Truth contained in the universal Buddha-Spirit'. Peering into that faded flower which never drew its strength from the River of God, it is hard to find any Jewel, but although inapplicable to the faith it is intended to epitomise, the phrase does in a way describe the physical situation of Kangting itself. Like the petals of a lotus flower the bare slopes of the mountains rise about the city, tapering to shapely peaks and serrated ridges far above. Nestling deep at their heart lies Kangting. Never shall I forget my surprise when, after travelling right across China and through its straggling, squalid cities, I found this veritable jewel hidden in the hills at journey's end. The streets were even made of concrete, and kept surprisingly clean. Main thoroughfares ran through the town from end to end and the laughing torrent tumbling through its heart gave a freshness and liveliness to the city quite unlike any other I had seen. Another surprise was to find that some enterprising committee had harnessed the local water power and the town was equipped with an excellent supply of electricity!

Our first few weeks in this entrancing border town were spent with several Christian friends* who kindly looked after us and helped us forward in every way. After this we were able to rent a Chinese house from a Tibetan landlord. It was set in a courtyard which we shared with several other families of different nationalities. Being able to speak some Chinese, it fell to me to set up our temporary home. When I entered the building I found it was being used to store some reeking, flea-ridden yak hides. Quickly disposing of these, I called in the local tradesmen and had the place whitewashed. I must say I was not too particular, so walls, ceilings, windows—in fact everything possible—was whitewashed, except the floors, which received a good scrub. The next thing was to get glass into the windows instead of paper, and to install some lighting. The landlord kindly agreed to get the boundary wall repaired if we would pay our rent in advance. Things moved forward smoothly so that within a few weeks all was in order—that is, all except 'the rats'. These required a separate strategy. Following a council of war one evening we trapped six one after another at quarter of an hour intervals. With these preliminaries

* Workers of the China Inland Mission.

dealt with we were now ready to begin the serious study of the Tibetan language.

Walking about the streets I was conscious that there were two kinds of institutions peculiar to the town. One was 'the caravansary' and the other was 'the lamasery'. As the terminus of the great Lhasa-India trade route, huge caravans poured into Kangting bringing scores of animals loaded with cloth, rugs, utensils, musk, furs, herbs, antlers, gold and even tiger claws! These animals with their packs would be led through the town to one of these numerous caravansaries. The dictionary describes a caravansary as 'a kind of unfurnished inn where caravans stop'. This is just what they were. Most of them had a big central quadrangle in which the animals would be received and unloaded. Around the quadrangle there was generally a continuous two-storeyed building. The ground floor was for stabling and storage, whilst the upstairs rooms were used to accommodate the traders and their men. Here they would stay for a number of days handling their business and disposing of their wares. Then they would purchase bales of tea, brought into Kangting from China. These they would sew up in wet yak skins to make sixty-pound loads and then one fine morning off they would go again into the vast interior bound, maybe, for Lhasa itself, a journey of some three months at 14,000 to 15,000 feet.

Though Kangting appeared at first like a jewel set in a lotus it was quickly brought to our notice that the town was blighted by an inward canker. The life of the caravansaries was essentially immoral. In these places where young girls served as maids it was almost impossible for any of them to remain pure, and diseases consequent upon promiscuity plagued most of the population. The lamasaries were possibly little better. These institutions, which were ostensibly places for the cultivation and propagation of the Lamaistic branch of the Buddhist faith, were open to grave abuses. Buddha, of course, means 'the enlightened one' and is the mystic title of Gotama, who founded the Buddhist faith some six centuries before Christ. He was a son of a chieftain pertaining to the small tribal group of northern India known as the Sakyas. Although surrounded with wealth and comfort he was deeply distressed by the sorrow and suffering around him. Eventually this conflict became so great that he renounced everything and wandered homeless and penniless in quest of that wisdom which would solve the enigma of human misery. After tasting all the teachings of his day he resolved to search out a new understanding of the problem of suffering by a sustained period of deep meditation. His theory, which later formed the basis of the new faith, came to him while he was seated under a fig tree which later was called the 'Bodhi-Tree'—the 'Tree of Wisdom'. It is from this word that his title of 'Buddha' is derived. Buddha believed that the law of cause and effect was the essential content of all phenomena. He came to the conclusion that suffering was 'the effect' arising out of one 'cause', namely desire. By continually diminishing our desirings, whatever they may be, the cause of suffering, issuing in such effects as 'discontent' uneasiness and irritability' would be ultimately extinguished. He thereupon propounded an eight-fold path, which was really a series of rules, to achieve this end. His teaching was not so much a religion but an ethical philosophy. He had no conviction that a supreme being existed, in fact he viewed all such considerations as irrelevant. He similarly repudiated the existence of a human soul as distinct from the human body. Although his teaching eventually spread over most of India and dominated oriental thought for many hundreds of years, this was far from being a personal triumph. His teaching only tended to emphasise the vast vacuum in human experience for which he himself could offer no provision. He left men without God and without hope in the world. Into this vacuum Buddha himself, together with his early disciples, was placed, being deified by his devotees. The original teachings of Gotama thus became much distorted and it was Buddhism in this corrupted form that became the religion of Tibet about six centuries after Christ. In Tibet at that time there was also the Bon religion, a belief synonomous with demon-worship. With this the degenerated Buddhism from India combined to form what is now known as Lamaism. These two strains of belief have continued through the centuries and are evidenced in the ritualistic and philosophic sects of the present-day lamas. To perpetuate a priesthood which would maintain a hold on the people approximately twenty, if not thirty per cent of all Tibetan male children were brought into this monastic system. As the lamas are obliged to remain celibate the entrusting of so many young boys to their 'tender mercies' creates a moral hazard second to none, especially under the auspices of such an evil system. Kangting was thus, quite literally, both a Sodom and a Gommorrah. Just outside the town lay a vast wilderness of rocks and boulders. A century or two previously one of the frequent earthquakes that shook the area split a wall of rock high in the mountains, to spill the waters of a lake into the valley below. In this way the first Kangting was destroyed. In our judgement it looked as if the second city was also heading for destruction, if not directly from the hand of God then through the poison of its own inherent vices.

During our stay in Kangting we visited most of the lamaseries in and around the town. The nearest one was about a hundred and fifty yards from where we lived. One day we took with us a bundle of Scripture portions in the Tibetan language and went in. A long shadowed passage led through into a broad paved courtyard. From the perimeter of this open space there rose high and imposing buildings. They were built largely of stone (although this is not always so) and along the sturdy walls were rows of tapering windows, each marking a lama's cell. The roofs curled outward and upward at the corners and on the highest pinnacle there glistened a ball of gold. Once our arrival had been noticed the lamas crowded round us, together with numerous boy novices. Their dress was a dull red serge sewn into a long drab gown, which draped them to the feet. There were no sleeves to this kind of robe but an extra piece of the material several feet long hung freely and was used to wrap around the shoulders. All the lamas, both young and old, were shorn of their hair, which only increased the austerity of their appearance. On their feet they wore the usual leather boot with the upturned toes. Unlike some of the lamas deeper in the plateau, those of Kangting were cosmopolitan enough to accept our literature quite amiably, although I must confess I never heard of any becoming Christians. There was another lamasery, similar to the one just mentioned, situated outside the town. On one of their feast days we visited the community there and George, by means of his earlier contacts with these lamas, managed to obtain an interview for us with the abbot and his assistant. The abbot himself bore every appearance of being a kindly old man. It was hard to believe that he ruled over such a sinister institution. My Tibetan was still poor, but finding he was bilingual I spoke to him in Chinese concerning Jesus Christ. The meeting was cordial enough. In fact it would have been quite disarming had it not been for the knowledge we had of the idolatry and superstition haunting the halls of this great fortress-like monastery. In its inner precincts stood their own temple, which housed a gigantic idol. How vacant are the faces of these images! These are the silent gods! 'They have mouths but they speak not; eyes have they but they see not; they have ears but they hear not; noses have they but they smell not. They have hands, but they handle not; feet have they but they walk not; neither speak they through their throat.'* And as from time to time we witnessed the lamas droning out their doleful liturgies; as we looked into their lustreless eyes and watched their feet tread the vain circle about their piles of graven stones we could only say, 'They that make them are like unto them; so is everyone that trusteth in them. O Israel, trust thou in the Lord'.*

The veneer of calm, serenity and even beauty that clings to some of the lamaseries is hard to overcome, especially when they are situated in sublime country that draws out the heart to God. One of the first excursions I ever made beyond the confines of the city

* Psalm 115.

was to a hermitage some hundreds of feet up on a neighbouring hillside. It was not a hard climb, and one afternoon we paid a call on the ageing lama who lived there. This man was much respected locally and we were interested to make his acquaintance. After quite a while we came in to a little dell, where we entered an enclosed courtyard. It was covered with short springy turf, and following the small stone pathway we approached the door of a single-story Tibetan house. As a retreat it was perfect. The town itself was obscured from view and no noise crept up from the valley. The tranquillity seemed to seep into one's soul. The garden was well kept and a short distance away on some weatherbeaten sticks a few prayer flags fluttered lethargically in the gentle breeze and warm sunshine. At the door the old lama greeted us. How genial he seemed, and so courteous as he welcomed us in. The interior of the house was equally tidy and well kept. The furniture was of good quality and the low couches and rugs extended round to a charcoal brazier on which rested the inevitable Tibetan tea-pot. He poured us out some buttered tea, the taste for which we had barely acquired, and we began to converse. Admittedly, there was some superstitious paraphernalia, and a few idols about the place, but in the dreamy setting of the hermitage high up on the hill they did not seem so offensive after all. Passivity is one of Buddhism's great emphases. Satan's hypnosis was being turned upon us. Why disturb these people? Why come from the ends of the earth to evangelise them? The sudden crack of the Divine Command awakened us: 'I send thee to open their eyes, and to turn them from darkness to light and *from the power of Satan unto*

God, that they may receive forgiveness of sins, and an inheritance among them which are sanctified by faith that is in me.'

By the time we had ridden the trails right into Tibet and had seen for ourselves the stark horror of the devil's work amongst this dying race, no pose of peace could hide from us the facts of war. 'We wrestle', says Paul, 'against principalities, against powers! Against the rulers of the darkness of this world, against spiritual wickedness in high places, wherefore take unto you the whole armour of God.'*

* Ephesians 6.

CHAPTER FIVE

NOMAD PUNDIT

BAY-MA was my teacher; and as he loped into my whitewashed room and took his place on a stool (something which was quite superfluous to nomad ease) he looked an incredible picture. His hair was one hideous tangle, around which was tied a coloured cord, complete with tassel hanging from the back of his head. His face was a smooth sallow brown, an appearance which was, perhaps, not altogether native to him. This strange texture of the skin was due to three if not four factors. First, of course, he was an oriental. The Tibetans are supposed to come of Mongol stock. Secondly, like most of the plateau-people, he did not believe in letting water come too often in contact with his face. At first I used to think this 'dirty' but later on I found it 'wisdom'. Once you face the bitter winds, biting frost and burning sun of Central Asia you think twice before washing your face. Thirdly, he quite likely had rubbed butter on his cheeks. The women go one better. They mix dung with it which, when dry, flakes off to leave little black flecks all over the face; something more attractive than might be imagined! Whether there were any other reasons I rather doubt, for he was one of those shrewd mountain folk who rarely drank spirits and who never touched opium. His robe, girt at the waist, was a matted grey-white garment made from wool spun in the tent. In all probability it had been washed even less than Bay-Ma himself, but then it must serve him both as a day-gown and a night-gown! Tibetans, you must remember, have never heard of pyjamas! His only other article of clothing was an ancient shirt which was preserved from looking too filthy by the fact that the neck which it encircled was so in harmony with it. On wet days, which were few in number because the rainfall of Kangting was only six or seven inches a year, Bay-Ma's appearance was even more bizarre. He would discard his high leather boots and appear with dripping feet, plus a big blue umbrella held aloft over his water-shy head. If you wonder at Bay-Ma's way of life, think for a moment of his background. Here is a man reared on the windswept grasslands and inured to the rough life of the hills. He tramps the snows, handles his yak and rides the ranges. He is of a virile nomad stock eking out an existence in a waste-howling wilderness known to the west as a 'lost horizon'. His is a life as rugged as it is ruthless, amongst a people whose only loves are feuds and horses, women and guns. Now he had come to town. For him this was a diversion, and to teach the foreigner, a kind of status symbol. As for the money that we could pay him, it probably meant very little. Had he not wives, and cattle, and influence beyond the passes?

So, like some wandering gypsy, he reported day by day. More often than not he would greet me with a broad smile and, with his face crinkling at the eyes, then give me a knowing look which was something more than just a 'wicked twinkle'. In one sense he was as naïve as a child but I soon found that as a man he was more mature than I. As for his knowledge of

Tibetan, little there was he did not know, whether one referred to the Lhasa or the Kham dialects, whether to the written or the spoken language, the classical or the vernacular. He was a man with a brilliant mind and head and shoulders above most in his own environment. Contact with Tibetans is one of those experiences that teaches you not to judge men by outward appearances.

Now the lesson begins. It is based on sentences taken from the fourth chapter of John's Gospel, a chapter, so say the grammarians, which contains practically every construction needful in the basic understanding of a language. "The women came to the well," Bay-Ma intones in his own tongue. I try to repeat it slowly after him. "The boy came to the well," he continues. I repeat the second phrase. "The girl came to the well," he says, and so it goes on. It is a ceaseless, merciless grind. With hard work, five years can make you a good Chinese speaker, but it takes ten to reach the same standard in Tibetan. The language is quite different from Chinese, being alphabetical. It may sound unbelievable but a month's hard study will enable you to read the written Tibetan. If you master the sounds of the letters and the peculiar but consistent spelling procedures (which extend above and below the basic letter of a word, as well as before and after it) then you can follow slowly along a line of Tibetan print even if you do not understand its meaning. The present script owes its origin to the old Sanskrit from which it was adapted in the seventh century. A man like Bay-Ma would have gained his knowledge from a scholarly lama, a few of whom do take the education of the rising generation seriously.

As the lesson drones on, Bay-Ma appears to lose

interest. His eyes and hands wander. Looking completely bored he picks up a magazine and scans the pictures. You feel he is failing in his duties, but suddenly his woolly head turns and he says quite decisively "Ma-ray," which is to say, "Not so" and, being corrected, one tries again. As the weeks go by we get past the woman and the well of John's Gospel, and begin to read steadily into Mark. Bay-Ma finds out who Jesus is. "Who was His mother?" he asks and, a little later, "Who was His father?" "His father was God!" I reply. This puzzles him, but it fits in reasonably with what he has already learnt, namely that Jesus is the Son of God, so for the time being he lets the matter pass.

Suddenly my concentration is rudely disturbed. As my eyes lift from the page I see a round bug, a brown one, about six inches away from me, clinging to the wall. I cannot detect Bay-Ma's initials on it but I have little doubt from whence it came. Bay-Ma, aware of the turn of my head, looks round and, following my gaze, spots the insect. He is unperturbed. Quickly I rise to kill it. At this Bay-Ma becomes very agitated and remonstrates with me. My action he feels is outrageous, especially as 'a teacher of doctrine'! Thoroughly aroused he forcibly restrains me from my purpose. Just at that moment somebody knocks at the door and as I leave the room I notice the offending creature has disappeared. Some time later I return and say to Bay-Ma in my limited Tibetan, "Did you find it?" "Oh, yes," he says, "I found it on the floor." "But where did you put it?" I ask. With great satisfaction he explains that he has taken it out to the verandah and let it drop down into the courtyard! "The life in that creature and the life in us," he says, "is almost the same." And then rather disconcertingly he adds "Would Jesus kill it?" It was one of those occasions most instructive to the missionary!

As I studied with Bay-Ma day by day, and he also became more acquainted with George and Gordon, we began to talk together about a visit to his part of the country. Such a venture would take us for the first time into the big grassland country of the plateau and introduce us to the nomad people. It would need quite a bit of organising but we felt it would be tremendously worthwhile. About that time we employed a rather doubtful character called Aily as our servant and he and Bay-Ma began to make arrangements. We looked on this as our first step on the road which one day would lead us to Lhasa. Over the months we gradually got together saddles, rugs, leather bags, tents, and utensils —in fact all the equipment necessary for a prolonged penetration into the high mountains of the plateau.

Although I was ultimately made a prisoner by the Chinese Communists when they marched into Tibet some two years later, the diaries of these early trips have been preserved. They remain a personal document of what was seen and felt when, as a young man still in my twenties, we were preparing to enter the Forbidden Land with the Gospel of Christ.

CHAPTER SIX

THE MINYA GONKA TRAIL

TURNING over the pages of my 1948 diary I came across the following entries. Suitably revised and edited for this record they run as follows:

Wednesday, July 28th. Weather good. Horses arrived about 1.30 p.m. We saddled three and told Aily to follow us as soon as the four yak were loaded. Bay-Ma, who was handling the hiring of the animals, was to accompany Aily. We passed out of Kangting by the southern valley, rode quietly by the two lamaseries on the west bank of the river and then broke into a fast canter. We gave the horses their heads in one brief gallop, but then settled down to the steady climb which will not slacken until we cross the 14,000 feet Jedo pass tomorrow. To the south I could see snow-covered mountains, their heads in the clouds. Within an hour we turned into another valley. It fell away from us as the roadway clung to the cliffs. We then encountered heavy rain, but by the time we reached Jedo, our first village, the clouds were breaking. We were now at an altitude of 10,500 feet. We took some tea in a very dilapidated dwelling, then leaving the house sat out in the open quietly meditating for the next hour. As the clouds lifted the magnificent spectacle of seven snow peaks in one unbroken range filled the horizon. There they stood, between 20,000 and 22,000 feet above sea level, an eloquent and united witness to the eternal power and Godhead of the One we serve. Somewhat after five Aily appeared in the distance, riding a horse and leading another, and from the way he motioned to us we knew he wanted us to proceed. We remounted and after about half a mile found a suitable place to camp for the night. Heavy rain fell again but the yak were not too long in coming and we pitched three tents without much difficulty. Our new Tibetan tent which Bay-Ma had designed and which a contact of his, an 'ani' (that is, a female lama) had sewn up, pitched excellently. Bay-Ma, Aily and the two yak-herds-women occupied this. Strange to us maybe—but to them not strange at all! I made a mental note, however, that an all-male party be engaged next time! First meal—fried eggs and sausages! It went down well! After supper played concertina and sang a bit round the fire. Read part of Colossians together and prayed. Felt very close to the four Tibetans with us. Barriers of race beginning to fade.

Thursday, July 29th. A fine dawn. Rose about 5.30 a.m. and had a time of stillness in the valley. Aily had breakfast ready by seven; rice, brown sugar, eggs and Tibetan tea. This doubtful liquid, which includes twigs as well as tea-leaves, he made in our wooden churn. This is a hollowed-out piece of tree trunk rather like a large edition of a Horlicks mixer, complete with wooden plunger. By eight o'clock we were on the trail again. A stiffening climb ensued through a wooded valley full of running streams, but by midday we emerged above the tree-line into a broad undulating area of grassland, where I had my first sight of a nomad tent. As we approached, two ferocious dogs bayed at us threateningly, but the occupants came out and having roped them to their stakes, welcomed us in. The tent was made of closely-twined yak or goats' hair and was of such a greasy texture that it let in the light without letting in the rain. Two Tibetan women were churning milk into butter in similar churns to ours but much bigger. In the centre of the tent floor was a fire with a cauldron hanging above it. Where the coarse canvas of the tent sloped down to the grass, odd things were stored serving as a wind-break, and I could see also several cakes of cheese stacked in a pile. Rough mats and skins were spread on the ground for us to sit on and several other nomads now slipped into the tent. They were all dressed in ragged sheepskin 'gowns', the woollen side of the fleece being worn next to the skin. Everybody seemed to be in good spirits and it was not long before Aily announced that tsamba (parched barley flour) was served. Buttered tea was poured into our bowls, handfuls of tsamba added and we tried to mix it without lipping any over the side, but alas we were still learners. I must say, to see dobs of butter floating around in the tea is not exactly appetising, but it is astonishing what you can get used to, especially on the roof of the world. A little of this tsamba keeps one going for hours on the road and is one of the chief factors, I am sure, accounting for the fine build of the Tibetans and their outstanding physical endurance. Between two and three in the afternoon we crossed the summit of the pass and dropping down several hundred feet entered a wide grassy valley completely deserted but for a few nomad tents. The country looked barren but seemed to beckon us. How welcome our intrusion, is hard to say, for on this very pass brigands waylay the unwary traveller and leave his skull impaled upon a post. Perhaps it is more than the demons that the Tibetans hope to placate as they toss a stone on the cairn, where the prayer flags flutter their tattered tails in the strong bleak wind. The sense of remoteness is amazing. Far away to the north I could still see mountains rising, lost in the blue of distance, whilst in the other direction the valley just tailed away. Within the next two hours we encountered vast herds of sheep and yak. Late in the afternoon we were confronted with another high ridge and the added altitude soon began to tax us. Gordon was feeling rough suffering from a stomach upset; I was sore with the unaccustomed riding, though George was still going well. Because of the failing strength of the horses we had to walk the last stretch to the top. Every few steps brought us to halt. Our party was rather strung out now but the herdswomen showed terrific stamina. Guiding the yak forward at a slow but constant pace they were at the crown of the ridge as soon as any. It was then I noticed for the first time that they were bare-footed! Beyond and below lay one of the most desolate places I think I have ever seen. Emptiness! It could have been a valley on the moon! As we set foot in it, however, we found that it was covered with vegetation, and the beautiful flowers which we had encountered much of the way continued. During the day I noticed such flowers as wild columbine, edelweiss, a kind of dog rose, types of gentian, forget-me-nots and primulas—a veritable botanist's paradise. Wild life, on the contrary, was strangely absent. It probably kept a safe distance from the trail; but leopard, tiger, bear, wild boar and even an occasional panda can be found in these mountains. The place where we camped we judged to be between 15,000 and 16,000 feet up and the erecting of the tents proved almost more than we lowlanders could manage. From somewhere the Tibetans produced a bundle of pinewood which, together with handfuls of the local scrub, soon kindled to a blaze. To watch them light a fire from a tiny spark struck off their tinder-box is an education in survival. The spark lodges in a piece of dry moss, is then fanned through pursed lips, planted in the fuel and blown up to a raging fire with goatskin bellows. These are completely open on one side but deftly closed with each descending stroke of the right arm. The extraordinary thing is that this fire-raising procedure is not a hit-and-miss affair. It works every time! After another supper of eggs and sausages we retired. It was only 8.15, but late enough!

Friday, July 30th. Attacked by huge black earwigs in the night and afflicted with a terrible headache in the morning. It did not abate until we descended the valley. I presume it must have been due to altitude. I still tried to begin the day reading in the Psalms but felt almost too sick to concentrate. Nevertheless I came to the great words, 'All the kings of the earth shall praise thee, O Lord, when they hear the words of Thy mouth'. How we long to see this fulfilled in the Dalai Lama and other high officials of Tibet confessing Christ! After a breakfast of bacon and eggs we mounted the horses and rode down the valley for about four or five hours. We passed an old fort, built of stone and clay, and along the trail saw some rodents rather like rats but the size of badgers. The weather was glorious and we had glimpses of snow-covered mountains through the clouds. Nomad encampments and herds of yak increased hourly. At 1 p.m. we set up camp in the midst of quite a nomad community. After some boiled beef and potatoes we got out the concertina and a cloth hymn sheet on which was written a Christian hymn in Tibetan. Quite a crowd gathered in and around the tent, and George was able to speak to them. As we expected to stay a few days in this area Bay-Ma has decided to visit his own valley not far away.

Saturday, July 31st. Still in the same location. A day of conversation with Aily the servant, hearing of his travels and learning of his background. Later we had about two hours on spiritual matters which he was eager to discuss. Using Chinese and Tibetan, Aily was able to understand fairly well what we were saying. George's Tibetan is better than mine and my Chinese is better than his, so between us we managed. It was an excellent time of personal contact with this man whom we hope will be of real help to us in both our travel and the work.

Sunday, August 1st. When I looked out of the tent shortly after six it was snowing and rather cold. After breakfast I practised the language, having a long conversation in Tibetan. Because we had no wine we decided in view of our short absence from Kangting not to have the Lord's Supper but it raised the question in our minds as to what we would really teach Tibetan Christians. There are no grapes grown here. The nearest thing perhaps to wine is their native beer made from barley. How important to keep the symbols in the right place and grasp the reality. Perhaps water would do, for that is what Jesus used when there was no wine. Why should we wonder when under His mighty hand water can turn to be wine indeed. Slept in the afternoon but managed to read much of the Scriptures in the course of the day. Very glad of the rest.

Monday, August 2nd. Rose 5.45 a.m. A faint covering of snow on the surrounding hills. Read the beautiful words in Psalm 141, 'Let my prayer be set forth before Thee as incense and the lifting up of my hands as the evening sacrifice'. About 9.30 a.m. Bay-Ma returned, bringing one of his wives with him. In addition to the promiscuity so prevalent amongst the Tibetans there are discernible three quite distinct forms of marital relationship in their feudal-type society. There is polygamy, of which Bay-Ma's married life is an example. There are some instances of monogamy, and there is also polyandry. This latter form is perhaps the one most distant from our Christian concept of family life. The way it works out amongst the Tibetans is that a woman will be married perhaps to three brothers. This in actual fact is not such an impossible situation as might at first appear, for one brother will likely be away at times in the hills herding cattle, another will sometimes go on a trading trip, whilst another will be responsible for the home farm. This means that only one brother is likely to be at home at any one time. As a system it provides the needed men to undertake the various tasks connected with the family's livelihood, and when it comes to offspring the substance of the estate is not dispersed between three families but is kept together and passed directly down through the first-born. Of course, it means that you do not ask a Tibetan who his father is; that causes embarrassment, but he will always be quite happy to talk of his mother. This particular wife of Bay-Ma who arrived today took charge of the yak, and the other nomad women went to their own valleys. We broke camp as soon as we could and headed up a long valley running at right-angles to the one we had descended three days before. We climbed solidly for an hour and a half, which brought us to a considerable elevation, probably to 16,000 feet once more. On reaching the crest we were rewarded with a breathtaking panorama. Beneath us there was the deep rift of a ravine, and then beyond it the country leapt up to well over 20,000 feet. Here and there glacier formations dipped down the scarred rocky furrows, but the utmost peaks were all enshrouded in cloud and we found it tantalising trying to imagine what the ridge-line would be if set against a clear blue sky. After the exhausting ascent we were careful to walk the horses for a while. However cruel to one another the Tibetans may be, they are always kind to their horses. 'Judge a horse by how it climbs a hill,' they say, 'and judge a man by how he comes down.' I never quite knew whether this was a question of physique only, or whether it extended to character. Certainly to ride a horse downhill was something they despised. Now the gruelling descent began. It lasted another one and a half hours and almost brought me to my knees. Then at the bottom, when I did at last re-mount and try to ford the rapids, my horse all but threw me in the water. I was glad to get to the other side still dry! We climbed a few hundred feet above the river and passed through low scrub which made the going difficult for the animals with loads. Another two or three hours' riding and we came to a kind of clearing where there was a solitary nomad tent, and here we decided to set up camp. A lot of firewood was stacked at the entrance flap. In fact the slit which permits access extends right back and serves as an outlet for the smoke from the fire; although it can be closed in stormy weather. Just inside the tent lay a little lamb. Butter churns and the indispensable cauldron were again in prominence and I saw some animal skins tied at the legs and filled with some commodity, probably butter. Skins make excellent containers, especially as glass bottles are virtually unknown. There was also a big copper vessel filled with water and this time I was conscious of a little god shelf. The idols were small but evidently reverenced. The man of the tent was away but a nomad woman busied herself here and there. She had two small children. One was about two, but whether boy or girl who could say? They all look the same with their tattered sheepskins, ruffled hair, and dirty faces. Then there was the tiny infant crying very bitterly. The little one, I think was rather unwell. There was also an older woman, whom I took to be the mother-in-law. The tent life of the nomads tends to be rather matriarchal but this poor soul looked mentally dull and sat silent. It was interesting to drop in on a nomad family and to see them just as they were. It took about an hour for the yak to arrive. After pitching our tent some distance away we piled up a great fire, for wood was more plentiful than we had known for days. Then under the night sky we sat talking with Bay-Ma, exercising our Tibetan, until the embers sank down into a dull red glow and we each went off to our tents.

Tuesday, August 3rd. Rose about 5.45 a.m. and picked strawberries on the hillside for breakfast. Had them with milk which we got from the nomad folk, plus some castor sugar we had brought with us. It came up with the last batch of stores sent in from West China.

Immediately after breakfast we broke camp. The ride was stupendous. We maintained and perhaps even increased our height until the chatter and laughter of the torrent below was lost in the abyss. The scrub turned to woodland in spite of the altitude and the woodland to forest. There were pines, holly trees, rhododendrons and a kind of ash. Some of the great areas of conifers flanking the hillside were eerie and ghostly. One whole section had been burnt out and the vast graveyard of lifeless trunks and leafless branches were like a host of skeletons on the march. Then we passed through another pine forest, deep in shadow where long green lichens and hanging mosses festooned the branches and caressed the face. It was like riding through one of those enchanted woods depicted in children's story books. As we emerged into the open again the scenery took on an even greater grandeur. The path narrowed drastically and became very perilous. I kept my right foot free from the stirrup much of the time as the horse only had to stumble and I would have gone falling headlong down the ravine. In fact it was a mercy I took this precaution. For one sickening moment the horse did lurch to its knees but, gathering up its feet, it took me on, still in the saddle. The familiar word of the Scripture, 'He keepeth the feet of His saints!' takes on a fresh meaning in Central Asia! After hours of riding along this trail we rounded the far extremity of the range and entered the Gonka valley, high up on the mountain slopes. We pitched our camp by the lamasery of the same name. The buildings were quite different from many of their kind, being in very poor repair and lacking the usual resident priesthood. It was fine to stretch our legs again and we allowed ourselves time for a quiet break before the evening meal. Somehow at this moment a depression seemed to seize hold of me and a sense of spiritual failure flooded in. Coming back to the tent I read Psalm 142: 'When my spirit was overwhelmed within me then Thou knewest my path.' Looking afresh to God, I found my resource in the quickening power of Jehovah. What great stamina is needed in spirit, mind and body to wage war against Satan in a land like this! A lama from the lamasery now came to see us and George talked with him, giving him a booklet in Tibetan entitled 'The Way of Salvation'. At night we sat round the camp fire, played the concertina and sang hymns and choruses together. Bay-Ma actually asked for the hymn on the sheet which we had had written out in Tibetan. It was the old favourite we have sung from earliest years 'What can wash away my stain? Nothing but the blood of Jesus'. These words seemed to hold a real fascination for him, and as his wife listened, you could see she was enjoying herself. Then we sang in English, 'Were you there when they crucified my Lord?' After we finished we could hear this nomad woman saying in English, "Tremble! Tremble! Tremble!" It was all she could remember of the refrain but she was a clever mimic and although she knew nothing at all of the English language, her pronunciation was perfect! After such a sing-song we retired later than usual. About 9.30!

Wednesday, August 4th. Rose approximately 6.30 a.m. and read a Psalm. 'Bow thy heavens O Lord and come down, touch the mountains and they shall smoke.' Breakfast of eggs, bacon and bread, all fried in butter. Butter is so plentiful here that even our mountain boots are oiled with it. It reminds me of Job who, when speaking of his abundance, said he washed his steps in it! Then, as breakfast finished, we literally lifted up our eyes unto the hills to see the amazing spectacle of Minya Gonka unveiled before us. Lofty ranges, rolling grassland, plunging ravines, stately pinewoods, running water, crystal-glaciers, twisting billowing cloud and alpine flowers at our feet but, Oh! there above all—that mighty glistening peak!! This indeed, was the end of the trail!

CHAPTER SEVEN

THE FAR HORIZONS

Thursday, August 5th. At 6 a.m. Bay-Ma's quizzical face peeped through the tent flap to say that Minya Gonka was again visible. He probably wondered why we foreigners should be so interested in the mountain but then 24,900 feet peaks are not so commonplace in the London suburbs! For the next two hours most of the mountain was visible, towering above us in all its elemental might against the azure blue. After breakfast Bay-Ma rounded up the horses and between ten and eleven we broke camp. The Gonka lamasery marks the farthest point of our present itinerary. As a first trip it is limited in extent being largely exploratory and experimental in character. As yet we are not really fitted for much direct evangelism amongst these people. We therefore returned on our tracks today, until we reached the nomad tent once more, where we had seen the young nomad children, and then, descending into the valley over very treacherous paths, we camped in a dry part of the river bed. There was a slight thunderstorm but we managed to get a camp fire going and Aily made some kind of bread on the red hot ash.

Friday, August 6th. I awoke early and going out into the fresh mountain air was greeted by a glorious dawn with snow-covered mountains stabbing their white fingers into the cold blue sky. We quickly got on our way and Bay-Ma found an excellent path enabling us to make good progress up valley, that is, until we crossed the river. On the farther side Gordon's horse tried to mount the steep slope rising from the water's edge but could only paw frantically at the clay, finding no grip. Slowly but inexorably it began to totter over backwards. Gordon tried desperately to retain his seat but all was to no avail. Horse and rider were thrown into the midst of the river! In the mercy of God however, Gordon managed to kick his feet free of the stirrups and so landed in the water clear of the horse. Thus, apart from getting a wetting, he escaped without injury. Walking briskly he kept himself warm in the exertion of the climb and gradually his clothes dried but it was hard going just the same. As for the horse, it was so unnerved that no sooner had we pulled it out of the river than it slipped and fell away down the bank into the water again. The next few hours brought us to an exceedingly high ridge. A well-known explorer of this area has estimated this range as 19,000 feet, but where we were standing must have been more in the region of 17,000 feet. Still, high enough when you have to climb it! We now descended and managed to contact the nomad community again, at the valley intersection known as Yulong-Shi. Aily bought fresh supplies from them and after a meal of tsamba and buttered tea we jumped into the saddle once more and aimed for the next pass, beyond which Bay-Ma's summer grazing grounds were to be found. It was another arduous climb to a great elevation. On the summit of the ridge there met our eyes the greatest mountain scenery I have ever seen. From horizon to horizon there stretched snow-covered peaks and ranges. Behind us rose Minya Gonka itself and before us, as far as the eye could see, there stretched for an immense distance, range upon range of hills and mountains like the heaving waves of the sea. Gordon took a compass reading. We were looking due north-west, right out across Central Asia in the direction of Chamdo. As I stood there in the loneliness of that breathless arena I felt it to be one of the greatest moments of my life. On the natural level I seemed like Columbus looking out across the Pacific for the very first time and, spiritually, like Moses on Pisgah surveying the Promised Land. My heart just surged out to the Living God—'O may we', my whole heart cried, 'be found worthy to possess this land. May there be no nomad camp, no city or hamlet across the whole of Central Asia where thine ambassadors shall not come.' My thoughts turned back through the years to the time when I stood in Carey's cottage in Leicester and vowed to my Lord that Tibet would be evangelised. Now I stood with the land before me. Deep emotions were still coursing through my soul as I began to descend the pass. On the lower slopes nomad encampments came into view again, and I found my heart going out to them as never before. Just a little further on, Bay-Ma's tents hove in sight. There were three altogether. Out ran a young lad and a nomad woman. They took our horses and off came the saddles. What a welcome they gave us! It was a lovely place, quiet and secluded. One could see the yak grazing on the mountain and the children enjoying the sunshine out on the grass. When I thought of all it meant to know Christ as my ever-present Companion, I looked at these folk living out here in this distant place and tried to imagine what it must be for them to be without Him. They pit as it were, their puny strength against these mighty mountains, facing alone the terrors and the tragedies of the Great Outdoors. All their life is a shadow-boxing with the demons and a losing battle with disease. What does it really mean to love these people for Christ's sake? And how can we put that love into action? Once the sun was down a cold, piercing wind swept across us from the snowy heights, but as I gazed upward at the darkening sky I saw the whole heaven fill with stars. Taking a pair of binoculars I went out and did some observing, seeking to identify the different constellations from this unfamiliar latitude. Maybe my astronomy will come in useful after all!

Saturday, August 7th. We have decided to stay the week-end at this camp site—I think Bay-Ma is pleased. During the morning we had quite a diversion. Bay-Ma came to Gordon with a sick yak. The eye was closing with a big ball of pus. This was an unexpected patient for us but a very valuable one as far as Bay-Ma was concerned. Having no medical training I could only look on, wondering whatever Gordon and George would do. First of all they gave the yak a dose of something(?). Then the poor beast had its legs trussed up, and with the brawny assistance of several nomads it was thrown to the ground. There it was held down on its back, with its long pointed horns dug into the earth. Prior to the operation three people were detailed to sit on its stomach. My name was called and I dutifully obeyed! Now with scalpel in hand, Gordon went to work. The deed was bravely done but I am glad it was the yak's eye and not the Bull's eye receiving the treatment! A dressing and drugs were immediately applied and for the first time in living memory a bandaged one-eyed yak roamed the slopes of the

Tibetan hills. Actually that is not quite correct—it was not even allowed to roam at first, but obliged to stand laconically, roped to a stake, until it knew how to conduct itself as an invalid!

After this episode things took a different turn. It seemed that western wonders must continue. Bay-Ma's wife came up and asked me to go to their tent to play the concertina. Several folk came in and my very limited repertoire received maximum appreciation. We now had an excellent opening. After they had enjoyed their fill of music, George produced a cryptic coloured poster. It was full of mystery to these nomad people. On the poster there were several drawings; a wooden cross, a crown of thorns, a spear and a whip and also a small picture of three crosses on a hill under a dark sky. Almost immediately the questions began to flow and George spoke to them as best he could about the crucifixion. With all these interruptions the work of the tents was coming to a standstill so two women and one of the boys broke away and began churning the milk in the wooden churns. As they worked the big wooden plunger, their hands deftly lifting the poles, they sang a Tibetan song, a weird chant which, as it was repeated again and again, haunted the mind. I tried to learn the tune, as I would like to collect some of the local melodies and set Christian words to them. There is no real Tibetan hymnology as yet in these parts. In the afternoon I meditated at length on Psalm 147. I wondered whether this Psalm had links with the post-captivity period, so commenced to read Ezra once again. After the evening meal the Tibetan folk asked to come into our tent. Two men and a boy, three women and a little girl came along. The concertina was again in vogue and Aily read and explained the Tibetan hymn sheet. The novelty of the words intrigued them greatly, not least of which was the word 'Hallelujah'! After we had finished they gave us a session of their own songs. They are vaguely reminiscent of some of our Hebridean airs. As we sat together in the shadows of the tent with the sound of their broken voices crooning in our ears, and their work-worn weatherbeaten faces illumined by the yellow light of a flickering flame, a sense of deep satisfaction filled my soul. We were in contact at last with the people to whom we had been sent.

Sunday, August 8th. Rose 6.30 a.m. Read remainder of the Psalms. Bacon and eggs again for breakfast but alas, we were out of bread! After breakfast had a long talk with Aily, who explained to me many things about hiring cattle, trading in the interior, etc., things very important for us to know once we are cut off from the outside world and penetrating far into the tableland. Gave the day largely to rest and meditation. The evening meal was in Bay-Ma's tent. He and his daughter partook with us of a specially prepared meal, a kind of mushroom soup which they eat with flour balls boiled in butter. We were not the only guests. Nine baby calves were also present, tethered in the other half of the tent!

Monday, August 9th. Broke camp early today, finally getting away from Bay-Ma's place shortly before 9 a.m. Once again our full complement of five horses and four yak were hitting the trail. We rode down the valley quite a distance until it broadened out and we could see it was extensively cultivated, although barley was about the only crop. Every four or five hundred yards there was now a clump of houses. They are flat-roofed fortress-like buildings, all looking most impregnable and ready for siege. Bay-Ma's winter house lay further down, but we did not visit it on this occasion. After a while we turned up alongside a tributary of the main stream flowing through the valley and eventually found ourselves by about three in the afternoon, looking out on a soft pastural scene of grassy hills, in places clad with fir. We camped on a flat patch of ground by a small brook trickling down through the rocks. I enjoyed a long and intimate talk with George before retiring.

Tuesday, August 10th. A ride of many miles but easy going most of the way until we topped a pass and descended across the shale slope of a mountain. This more treacherous part of the trail brought us down into one of the valleys which had led us towards Minya Gonka. By mid-afternoon we had commenced the descent to Jedo but decided to sleep in the open one more night rather than try to make the village by dusk. Towards evening one of Bay-Ma's wives became agitated. I did not see what was the matter at first, but she was obviously fearful of some impending danger. Bay-Ma took his revolver and quietly slipped away from the camp. He made his way silently downhill a short distance and then I noticed first one man, and then another, coming stealthily up the valley. It looked as if we had encountered some highly dubious characters. Watching from a distance I waited to see what would happen. Although one hears of banditry it is hard to think of anything really happening to us. As the men approached, Bay-Ma seemed to identify them and disclosing himself he went towards them.

There was apparently no hostile intent. They had been as doubtful of us as we had of them. So we slept peacefully that night after all, there being no further incident.

Wednesday, August 11th. Rising early we took our last breakfast of the trip and then mounting our horses rode ahead of the main party. We were soon passed, however, by Aily riding fast into Kangting in order to prepare for our arrival. In about two hours we were in Jedo. Turning off the track we went up the mountainside for some distance to a hot sulphur spring. This whole region of Central Asia is thermal. The water was too hot, but by diverting a cool stream into the pool we were able to make it tepid enough to bathe in. It was a novel experience lying up to the neck in hot sulphur-water looking at 20,000-foot snow peaks across the valley. When we came out the sun was so hot we hardly needed to dry ourselves. We quickly dressed, jumped once again into the saddle and then at a sharp trot posted all the way back to Kangting. The simple whitewashed house looked like a palace after living in tents so long and as far as the town was concerned it really did seem like 'the outside world'. Collecting the mail I read it hungrily, thankful to God for a great trip, a safe return and news of loved ones far away.

CHAPTER EIGHT

NUMBER EIGHTEEN, RADIANT LIGHT STREET

RADIANT Light Street was the illustrious name inscribed on the official plaque attached to our wooden Chinese house in the Tibetan border town of Kangting. Actually Radiant Light Street was not a street at all. It referred, as far as I could see, to a straggling series of buildings erected without plan or consultation along the banks of a millstream; and in this sense I suppose the stream was the street. From a small footpath edging the stream you could step through a walled gateway into the courtyard between two houses. One was Number Eighteen which we rented and the second another number which I do not know. By the time we had whitewashed the inside of our house and fitted up the electric lighting the general impression of the place came a little nearer to its official name plate. Even so a lot transpired within that compound which could never stand the light. Our strenuous days of study were consequently punctuated with many a fearful and tragic event.

First let me tell you about our neighbours. In 'the numberless house' sharing the courtyard, numberless people came and went. It was occupied by various families. In one of the ground floor rooms lived two elderly women of doubtful nationality. They were poor, ragged old souls, and they had a hard time of it because for years and years people had been cutting wood around Kangting until all the nearby slopes were completely denuded of worthwhile tinder. They had therefore to rise early, walk several miles, and then after hacking away at the very tough scrub in the mountains, strap the sticks on their shoulders and trundle them all the way in to town. The remaining front room had earlier been occupied by another woman whom we never really came to know. Her husband had recently died, or been killed on the road outside Kangting, and shortly after we moved in the Taoist priests were called. In they sauntered with all their 'sounding brass and tinkling cymbals' and you never heard such a woeful, devilish going on of gong-clanging, dirge-singing and raucous incantation. From time to time paper money (not the real thing, of course, for the priests would pocket that) was burnt in the courtyard under the superintendence of the chief priest, whilst the courtyard wall smoked steadily with a battery of joss-sticks giving off a heavy fragrance. In the midst of all this the bereaved woman would bow at times to the ground in the middle of the courtyard. It was pitiful to see her. In the back rooms of the house lived another family. I think they were Tibetan although the father was more like a tribesman. His wife was a bright hardworking person but the man himself rather lazy; an attitude he no doubt deemed the male's oriental prerogative. They had two fine children, a boy of fifteen and a girl of about thirteen. In the setting their moral prospects were hardly bright, even though they lived in Radiant Light Street. Upstairs on one side lived an old man and his better half. He was an occasional water-carrier and his wife a woodcutter. He was a gruff old fellow but quite kindhearted once you got past his voice. In the last room of the house lived an ugly young woman of very doubtful livelihood. She wore good clothes in what were otherwise very poor surroundings, and had soldiers of the National Chinese Army running up and down stairs all times of day and night. These were our neighbours. The courtyard also sheltered a monkey, a pig, two cringing dogs and a bounding puppy. In addition to these lowlier occupants, there were times when our horses also enjoyed standing room. Such then was Radiant Light Street!

Late one night, long after dusk, there was an unearthly din in 'the numberless house'. We quickly put the light on in the courtyard and ran across to see what was happening. The sound was coming from one of the back rooms. Shining a torch through the wooden lattice-work we peered into the dark interior. A scene of utter confusion met our gaze. Furniture lay upended all over the floor; and what was more ominous, acrid fumes caught at our throats. At first we could see little more than the tiny flame of some butter lamp, but then to our horror we saw the big tribesman lurching grotesquely about, with his wife dishevelled and almost unrecognisable at his feet. As he began to strike her again we knew that a few moments might see her bludgeoned to death. She tried to raise herself but her husband grabbed hold of her and flung her once more to the ground. We made a bee-line for the front door, and in a matter of seconds we had found our way through the darkened house to the scene of the murderous activities. By the light of the torch we cautiously approached the man whose top teeth gnawed and slobbered at his lower lip. Something needed to be done and done quickly. In the fury of his attack he had knocked over the charcoal brazier and sent the hot cinders sprawling all across the wooden floor. The place would be ablaze in a matter of minutes. The sudden entry of three young Europeans seemed to arrest his attention. George went quickly forward and I watched, expecting every moment to see the frenzied man pound his fist into George's face, but God restrained him. The man seemed almost hypnotised. George stared him straight in the eye and without lowering his gaze extended both his hands, until his fingertips gently touched the man's sleeves. Then, still looking him through and through, he drew his fingers downwards until he quietly gripped his wrists. Suddenly the man became like a little child. Gordon deftly passed an emetic over his lips and together they led him outside whilst I coped with the crisis in the house. It was difficult to know whether the man was demon-possessed, intoxicated with the local fiery liquor or both. We hardly saw any of the family for the next two days. Later on they all turned up again and the now-sober tribesman, meeting us along the road, walked with his tongue hanging out for almost fifty yards! By way of explanation, this is the Tibetan way of showing respect to a superior. It was only the mercy of God that prevented us from injuring him that night of his débâcle. Whether he remembered the kindness shown I do not know but we seemed to have won a way into his heart and perhaps that was the first step towards winning him for Christ.

We now seemed in the thick of it. Aily was caught out in an underhanded deal and had to be relieved of his duties. Then Gordon, whom we had hoped so much would work with us in Tibet, married and felt it preferable to leave the border and go to India. In addition to this I began to have the most strange and unnerving experiences at night. I believe at this time we were only just beginning to realise the sinister forces operating against us. Missionary work in the minds of young people can too often be viewed as a life-long Cook's tour with occasional preaching thrown in. We forget it is a battle against the cruellest and most unprincipled of foes. This we may admit theologically but are slow to realise until the tempo of the battle quickens; and it was quickening now. I hardly know how to describe what happened on those frightening occasions. In the small hours I would half wake up to find myself either 'climbing the wall' or else crouching doubled up on the floor at the foot of my bed. To me it was something more than mere sleepwalking or a nightmare. It was molestation by some unseen evil force. The climax came when one night I walked right through two rooms in my sleep, struck a window, knocked the glass out, then returned to bed. When I awoke in the morning I was aware I had broken the glass but could account for little else. In the midst of language study, living at a high altitude and subject to the current pressures, it was conceivable I might have some restless nights, but in all my adult life I could not recall having such experiences. I confided in George, who himself became concerned at what was happening. We felt our only recourse, in view of such disturbing symptoms, was to make it a definite matter of prayer. We had heard of Tibetans who, after professing to trust Christ, had had experiences not dissimilar to my own.

One such case in Kangting had culminated in the man's tragic death. These were matters we could not understand but in the circumstances tended to heighten our apprehension. One day I looked at the doorway of my bedroom. Whether I had noticed it previously or not I cannot remember, but there, carefully drawn, or perhaps one should say tattooed on the wood, was one of the mystic letter-formulas of Lamaism. Somehow deep within me I felt a sense of association between the molestation I was experiencing and this sign drawn upon my door. I mentioned it to George, whereupon we literally cut it out of the wood. From that time I experienced no further interference of these evidently Satanic forces. It was a lesson to us concerning the fearful and challenging task to which we had been called. If one examines the history of those who have sought to enter Tibet it is significant to notice that many, if not all of those who have presumed to go up against these gates of evil, have been mauled in one way or another by the very talons of the devil. In my own case I had no inkling at that time how severe that mauling was ultimately to be.

There is a day in the life of any missionary which is at once the most 'terrifying' and yet in a way the most thrilling. That is the day when he gives his first real talk in the language of the people to whom God has sent him! It was only a year or so previously that I had given my first talk in Chinese. That had been to Chinese children. This had been followed by an opportunity of speaking to a Chinese crowd in a street in Siushui in Central China. Talk of Belshazzar and the writing on the wall! If ever my 'knees smote together' they did that day! What a humiliating yet exhilarating moment.

My worst howler in Chinese was to have all the guests at the marriage in Cana taking doses of medicine instead of drinking wine! Now in my faltering Tibetan I had to face the same ordeal all over again. Both George Patterson and I owed much under God to the instruction and encouragement of a Mr. George Kraft, working amongst the Tibetans on the border, and it was under his leadership that we were now venturing to make the Gospel known in this difficult tongue. I opened the meeting with the hymn 'We have heard the joyful sound, Jesus saves'. One of our teachers had written out the words in big Tibetan print. In front of me sat a motley group of Tibetans. Generally speaking it took five or six Chinese to fill one of the benches but once the nomads came in and sat down surrounded by the massive folds of their sheepskin gowns, then three were ample. Whether they understood anything that first night I rather doubt but at least I had made a beginning!

It was in the course of this work that we first made contact with Dopgyay of the house of Pangda. One night when trying to get Tibetans in to the meeting George spoke to a well-to-do Tibetan accompanied by his servants and to his surprise the Tibetan turned in to hear not so much, I should imagine, what the foreigners were saying but how they were saying it! This initial contact, plus the fact that George was able later on to treat him and his family medically, led to a very real friendship with this man who proved to be a key figure in the political upheavals of the time. This he brought home to us very strikingly on a similar occasion. It was pitch dark when we left the meeting to walk the short distance to his compound. Having a torch with us we shone it in the street. "Put it out!" he suddenly snapped. "Remember they can see us but we can't see them!" And it was not long before we knew what he was talking about.

CHAPTER NINE

WHERE SHADOWS FALL

DOM-NAG was the name of our dog. 'Black bear' was its meaning and if ever a dog was a bear, and a black one at that, then that dog was Dom-Nag! He hailed from across the road, where lived a local aristocrat named Jah. This man was in touch with Lhasa yet also had his hands on Chinese affairs. We had good contact with him and he took no little interest in what we were doing. He even forwarded, with his own recommendation, our application to the Tibetan Government for permission to work in that country. Because of medical help given to his family he gave us Dom-Nag. This beautiful but vicious animal we chained to the wall of the courtyard and one could only pity the thief who came within striking distance of those sabre-toothed jaws. To us who fed him he was like a lamb. We could do anything with him. He was so big that when he stood on his hind legs his paws rested on our shoulders. Dom-Nag was really magnificent and we looked forward to the day when we could take him on our journeys.

In China events were moving swiftly towards their climax. City after city fell before the Communist armies, and Kangting, although so far away from the actual conflict, tended to reflect the moods and unrest of the times. Life in this border town became more and more uncertain and we never really knew when rioting between the Tibetans and the Chinese would break out. It was at a time like this that a message came in from the grasslands to tell us that the old mother of George's teacher was dangerously ill. As Bay-Ma also had affairs requiring attention in the nomad country it seemed most opportune to take another trip. Very quickly Bay-Ma produced nine yak from where we did not quite know, and as we ourselves now owned four horses, within a day or two we were once again heading out of town towards Jedo and the passes. We formed quite a procession marching past the Chinese customs post. In addition to the two teachers, two herdsmen, one of Bay-Ma's wives, our two selves, the horses and the yak, there were also two young calves, three piglets and, of course, this time the pride of our party, Dom-Nag himself!

It was already November, and as we climbed we saw a marked change in the countryside compared with summertime. Iron frosts at night, streams frozen almost to the bottom, and heavy trudging through snow fields were some of the great differences from those more lazy days when there were alpine flowers and green grasses all the way. On this trip, owing to the intense cold of the early morning, we tended to rise later. As one rode along, the leg on the shadowed side would be frozen stiff, whilst the other was roasted in the sun. It was essential to shade one's face with a wide-brimmed hat, otherwise the skin was dreadfully burned and one ended up with a big ugly scab on the nose. The eyes, too, had to be shielded with dark glasses or snow blindness quickly set in. The Tibetans, I noticed, pulled down their long black hair over their eyes, but even then they could suffer terribly before we descended out of the snow into a lower valley. The scenery seemed now even more stupendous and the Tibetans with us even more rugged. In spite of the intense cold they would not bestir themselves to pitch a covering canvas but preferred to sleep in the shelter of the loads stacked about the camp fire. It was not their custom, they said, which is their unfailing means of resisting all innovation; but toughening to the open life though we were, we still felt it more 'customary' to pitch a tent! For several days we travelled flat-out, riding and trekking through a frozen but sunbathed waste, to reach the teacher's old mother ere she died.

Four days out from Kangting we descended into a valley well below the tree-line, and there came across the first extensive signs of human habitation. We were now approaching the teacher's community. George's tutor, from the beginning, we always called 'Gigen', which itself means 'teacher'. It seemed to fit him so deservedly, for he was the most scholarly of all the Tibetans we employed during our time of language study. In his younger days he had been secretary to a monastery but later had married and on this account had been obliged to renounce his position. It was only after a prolonged period of hardship that he eventually established himself as a teacher in Kangting. In spite of his 'delinquency' he was, however, a faithful Buddhist and although very knowledgeable in the Christian New Testament his old loyalties firmly held him still. From day to day I again kept a diary and we pick up the story now from this old record . . .

Saturday, November 6th. By lunchtime we reached a series of fortlike feudal dwellings owned by some of Gigen's relatives. We dismounted and were quickly welcomed inside one of the big stone-walled courtyards. A dog resented our intrusion with Dom-Nag-like ferocity, but I was relieved to spot its chain. We passed through a large wooden doorway into an unbelievably dark interior. This was accentuated by our coming in out of the sunshine. As one's eyes became accustomed to the gloom I could see that we were standing in a kind of baronial hall, and that such light as there was, came slanting through small squarish windows set at intervals along it. At one end of the room was a huge open hearth on which a dung and log fire was burning under a massive cauldron. Tibetans sat squatting around it. We joined them and shared their meal of tea and tsamba. The smoke from the fire passed up through a cavern-like hole in the middle of the house. The wooden beams and pillars supporting the ceiling were all coated with a kind of tarry substance and the walls panelled with wood halfway up. Above the woodwork on the mud facing were scrawled symbols like the antlers of a deer, marks which I felt had some superstitious, rather than ornamental significance. Skins containing food hung here and there. I noticed a gun, too, and at the entrance a big prayer wheel. These prayer wheels are really leather cylinders containing innumerable pieces of paper on which are written the words 'Om mani padme hum'. Guests are expected to flick the cylinder round as they come and go, and thus ensure that each of these prayers is freshly launched against the unseen world of demons. It was my first time in such a dwelling. I found it intensely interesting but very dark. Indeed that was my deepest impression. *It was very dark.* After lunch we pressed on down the valley to another hamlet where we camped for the night. The frost was much less severe and after the very demanding travelling of the past few days, it was lovely to go out in the brilliant moonlight and commune with God. Gradually the sense of exhaustion receded and the eternal perspectives re-emerged in my tired mind.

Sunday, November 7th. Although we broke camp and packed our boxes, we could not get away. A girl arrived with a rat bite on her neck. This took time to dress and it was as late as 10.30 before we were on the trail. As we passed through a Tibetan village I spotted three young goats and before I could do anything Dom-Nag was after them. I was sure he would kill them but meanwhile we could only ride on. To our consternation no Dom-Nag appeared, so I was obliged to go back to the village and see what damage had been incurred. Eventually I found not the dead kids but almost a dead dog. The incensed villagers had stoned and beaten Dom-Nag to within an inch of his life. At first I could hardly get him to stand he was so stunned, but after a while he recovered sufficient strength to walk. He was bleeding at the mouth and his eye, too, was cut but I left without protestation lest they stone me also! At almost every step now the medical box was in demand and I began to see how very sick the population was. All down the trail we saw gold diggings. They were mostly Chinese workings but few had 'struck it rich'. A little further on I saw my first water-driven prayer wheel. The big cylinder of Buddhist sayings was kept revolving by a mountain stream. It would be hard to imagine anything at once so ludicrous or pathetic as this mechanical religious device. Another hour and we passed a big lamasery. There it stood, high on the hillside above us, its white walls rising like battlements against the blue of heaven. About a mile beyond it we came to Gigen's village.

Gleeful, dirty youngsters came racing out to greet us. We were immediately relieved of our animals and taken through ground-floor stabling and up to the third floor of this castle-like dwelling. Our room contained three or four low Tibetan tables with spacious rug-covered dais to match. There was a charcoal fire, a cupboard, and behind our sleeping couch were latticed windows covered with paper. As we settled in, Gigen came into the room to say that his mother's condition was very low so we went down immediately to the big living room on the second floor. It was very similar to the one encountered up the valley. Outside the daylight was almost gone and although there was a blazing fire on the hearth it seemed to add little comfort to the darkened room. A Tibetan woman brought a flare of pine chips and groping our way over to a murky corner we discerned an old Tibetan lady lying on a pile of ragged bedclothes. George took out his stethoscope, sounded her and felt her pulse but it was not discernible. She was in a dropsical condition and the water was almost to her heart. Seeing the grave look upon his pupil's face, Gigen quietly said in his native idiom, "We Tibetans have no way for her". It was a situation fraught with disturbing possibilities. If we could not relieve her then our God would be deemed as impotent as theirs. If we attempted to give her a specific drug, in her great weakness she might die immediately. George turned to me, and said in English, "We will pray first", then speaking in Tibetan he told Gigen and the others crowding round what he intended to do. "We are going to pray to God," he said. Closely they watched and listened and, true to His promise, God Himself drew near. As soon as George had finished, he gave the old lady a maximum dose of a drug we had brought with us. The effect was quite wonderful. In a few minutes her breathing changed for the better and she settled to the best night's sleep she had had for a very long time. The teacher sat on with his mother and we went over into the firelight to squat down beside the family. There was one very aged man with glassy eyes counting his rosary. Beside him sat a woman of about sixty, totally blind, whose sole occupation was the turning of her prayer wheel. Next to them played a lively little boy of about four, who as the room grew hotter ran about stark naked, the firelight dancing on his grubby little brown body. Then there was his mother, a striking young woman who sat beside the menfolk, one of whom was leisurely smoking a long pipe. We talked with them for a while then returned to our room upstairs. One by one they followed us until Gigen also came. When all were present he took out the presents he had brought from far-away Kangting, that 'great metropolis' of the outside world! Amongst the gifts were some coloured pictures, very wonderful to Tibetan eyes and, best of all, a whistle for the little boy! But the surprises were not finished yet. He showed them now photographs of the town and these just completed their evening. As they left us, we climbed into our sleeping bags and my mind reached out across the seas and continents to England. It would be Lord's Day morning there and my dear ones at home would be sitting at the table of our Lord.

CHAPTER TEN

A HERMIT'S TEARS

OUR stay in the teacher's valley continued several days. My impressions recorded at the time continue in the following vein.

Monday, November 8th. It was about ten minutes to seven when I woke up so I arose and went out on to the flat roof where the presence of God refreshed my soul in the light of the dawn. We breakfasted at 8.30, entertained by these hospitable folk on the fat of their land. Never have I seen such milk and butter! We shall have to call a halt somewhere! After breakfast I did some book-work on the language, continuing in Mark's Gospel. It was not long though before a very sick woman arrived suffering from T.B., who also needing a gaping wound bandaged. Numerous folk began to gather about us, and later in the morning, I explained to them what I had been studying in the Gospel. Some distance away there was an old man listening and I asked him whether he had heard this news before. Apparently it was the very first time he had heard of Jesus. Later in the day Gigen showed us round the house. It was a building of considerable proportions. He took us first to a huge store-room stacked with artistically painted chests. There were also a number of large cupboards, for this was the place where the ornaments and robes worn on special occasions were all carefully stacked away. Next we were taken to the family shrine. In this room there was a huge idol and many volumes of the Tibetan classics. These looked peculiar to our eyes, being loose-leaf tomes about two feet long and five inches wide. The ageing yellow sheets lie between thick wooden boards and are bound up with ribbon when not in use. As we scanned the idolatrous paraphernalia, Gigen said apologetically, "This is a Tibetan custom, do not be offended". Looking a little closer we saw that one whole wall of the room was devoted to the chief idol and its attendant effigies, whilst the other three walls were exquisitely adorned with various other 'deities'. The floor was covered with blocks of wood all carefully inlaid. It was obvious that neither time, effort nor expense had been spared in their attempt to propitiate the gods of their religion. In this room one of Gigen's lama brothers had his sleeping-couch. The evening turned out to be a time of boisterous humour for one of the most hilarious of Tibetan characters dropped in to see the family. He was deaf and dumb but mentally brilliant. He was another of the teacher's brothers and having grown up with this household all knew how to make him understand. To see this crowd of Tibetans gesticulating and grimacing in this quaint fashion was an unexpected entertainment! The deaf and dumb man enjoyed it most of all. He dominated the whole group; and we were told that by reason of his amazing ability to communicate he was able to carry on a cattle business without any real difficulty.

Tuesday, November 9th. After a morning of Tibetan study and opportune conversation we had something of a dispensary session on the flat roof of one of the village houses. For the first time in my life I saw venereal disease in all its vileness. The case in hand was that of a young woman of twenty-six. Perhaps she was more sinned against than sinning, but the sight of such putrefaction was utterly ghastly. There is every evidence that ninety per cent of this robust race are tainted in some degree with this appalling disease. It affects their teeth, their eyes and their limbs, indeed one feels that much of the illness encountered stems from this dreadful thing. Within the limits of our ability and the medicines at our disposal we did what we could. The sunshine streamed down benignly as we worked on the roof top. Surely an emblem of the grace of God lavished so abundantly on all kinds and conditions of men.

Wednesday, November 10th. At 11.30 we went with Gigen to visit his old lamasery, the one we passed on our way down the valley a few days before. It was a strenuous walk for we were probably still over 10,000 feet. After quite a toil up the hillside we came to a cemetery, bedecked with washed-out prayer flags and a monument called a chörten. These are peculiar erections shaped like inverted tulips. They are sometimes very big and are really whitewashed sepulchres of famous 'saints'. No sooner were we beyond the chörten than we had our first glimpse of the lamasery. It was of considerable size and surrounded by a number of lesser buildings. Some of these were very well built. They had highly-coloured window pieces and decorative friezes lining the eaves. Large stones were set at intervals on the sloping sectors of the roofs, to prevent damage from high winds. Its physical situation was sublime. There was no other word for it. The main block commanded a glorious vista of the mountains and took in a grand sweep of the valley below. Gigen led us in, across the main quadrangle flanked by the lamas' three-storey living quarters. On our left an ornate doorway marked what was, presumably, the major shrine, and above the curved extremities of the roofing three golden pinnacles glittered richly in the sun. The treasurer, who normally would have received us, was away in Kangting but his apartments were open and placed at our disposal. Had Gigen not defaulted he would probably be occupying these very quarters. We were asked to sit down on the low couches and were served with buttered tea. Many of the young lamas gathered to see us, curious to know why we had come and what we were going to do. As we refreshed ourselves George distributed some Tibetan leaflets concerning our Lord Jesus Christ. "This is God's teaching," he said. "Don't use it as paper to stick over the cracks in your doors and windows. That would be a great sin and receive God's punishment!" At this pronouncement they seemed a little awestruck but they thawed a bit when three sick folk received medical examination. George now attempted to preach but stopped when it became evident that they were not yet prepared to give us serious attention. They were, I think, the most highly-spirited group of teenage lamas we had ever met. It so happened their superiors were away that day! We now went outside and Gigen led us to a small house on the hillside which was a hermitage. Here lived yet another of his brothers, a lama of no mean reputation who had shut himself away for meditation. Apart from the little boy-monk attending him, this man as far as we knew had already been in complete retreat for several years. News recently came through to Gigen that he was failing in health, and on this ground alone was it thought that a visit from the foreigners-with-medicines might be permissible. When the moment for our entry came, we slipped in quietly to the hushed precincts of the hermit's room. I wondered greatly what kind of person this man would prove to be. There he was in his long red priestly garb sitting crossed-legged before three low Tibetan tables. The little lama servant boy was just making some cakes and brewing tea. We were motioned to sit down on the stools provided. My eyes began to take in the contents of the chamber where this lonely mysterious figure lived. Behind him on the wall was a series of sinister black pictures depicting, as far as I could judge, stages of intercourse with the nether world. On his right were various Tibetan books bound up in their boards, each with an orange sash. From the ceiling hung a variety of prayer flags. They were attached to each beam and spaced a few inches apart. I looked closely at the man in front of us. He began to speak with his brother Gigen and then turned to George. I had somehow imagined he would be strong-willed and nervously robust, but I was disillusioned. The poignant nature of the occasion affected the old lama profoundly and to my amazement he began to weep. He was not a strong man, after all, but broken and distraught, haunted no doubt by the terrors of the spirit world around him. He was most anxious to obtain a medicine that would effect a cure. "And why do you want it?" George asked. "Is it for your head, or your stomach . . ." and he mentioned various other parts of the body. "No," he said, "it is for my mind." "For the mind there is only one answer," George replied. "You need to believe in

Jesus." Ere we departed we left him a number of Scriptures. They contained enough of the Bible in his own language to point him all the way to heaven and I had little doubt in his loneliness he would read them again and again. As we turned towards the door we perceived the basic reason for his tears. Set in the wall opposite the lama was a tiny idol, whether of gold or stone I cannot say. Before this pathetic fragment of material he had placed his pitiful offerings. Day after day and year after year, his gaze had been focused and his faith centred in that wretched thing. He had looked too long in the wrong direction; he had worshipped too long the wrong god and now at the last it was breaking him to pieces. Could it be in the quietness of his room this man would turn from idols to the living God? Slowly we wended our way down the mountain. Numbers of young lamas followed us, some of whom we had seen earlier. Mustering quite a band of them I told them I would take their photo, something which greatly intrigued them. Once it was taken they were ready to listen to what I had to say and I gave them the fullest presentation of the Gospel in Tibetan I have managed so far. We reached Gigen's village just before sundown. The meal was taken in our own room together with Gigen, his resident lama-brother and the steward of the house. The conversation turned almost at once to spiritual matters and there followed quite a profound and penetrating discussion. George handled this most of the time and as the lama lost ground and became confused, he sighed sadly "My mind is like a yak's mind!" Their idea of debate is a religious exercise in which you score points, and they love to bring one hand down upon another when they feel they have made a clear advance over their opponent. But what is the good of winning an argument and losing your soul! Whether the lama was just disheartened at not getting the conversation all his own way or perhaps, deeper down, disturbed by his unpreparedness to meet 'The Elevated One', as they sometimes inadequately describe the Supreme Being, it was difficult to say. Gigen I think, too, was much sobered. He often pondered the Christian faith, but as far as we know has not as yet in any way yielded to the claims of Jesus Christ.

Thursday, November 11th. Rose about 6.45 and enjoyed a meditation in Luke's Gospel. Breakfast was barely over when sick folk began to arrive. After they had been cared for and the morning sunshine had spread right across the valley floor, I went out on to the roof to butter my boots and also my sheepskin jacket, which had dried out through our travelling in the sun. As I worked away there on the roof I began to converse with an intelligent young man repairing his gown. I was greatly taxed by reason of my limited Tibetan, but he was so vitally interested in what we had come to teach that he seemed to grasp very quickly what I was trying to say. He was anxious to know whether we had three gods or one. "Because," he said, "we also have three gods. We have Buddha; then we have the whole canon of the Buddhist scriptures, (taken by some to be one hundred and eight volumes), and then in addition to these we have the whole body of the Buddhist priesthood. These are our three gods. What are yours?" There now ensued a most fascinating talk together concerning the Godhead, and as I sought to tell him of the Father, the Son and the Holy Spirit, largely by means of simple illustrations, he was most attentive. Before we parted he gladly received a copy of Mark's Gospel in Tibetan. Later in the day, George and I went for a walk across the wooden cantilever bridge to the farther side of the valley. A whole band of ragged youngsters between the ages of five and nine followed us and we had a great time with them throwing stones. The accuracy of the children's aim was astonishing. We were no match for them at all!

Day by day George has been tending Gigen's mother. She has been responding favourably to the drug given her, but as we propose going tomorrow he felt that the medical facts of her condition should be intimated to Gigen so he might be under no misapprehension regarding the critical condition in which his mother lay. He therefore told him that we had done all that we could in the circumstances. It seems that this was taken as an excuse for getting the lamas back and this afternoon the incense-burning was recommenced. George reproached himself greatly for this, although I could hardly see that he was to blame. Gigen tried to pass off the matter saying that our work and the lamas' was after all the same thing, but I remonstrated with him in front of his people and after a bit of sidestepping and face-saving he eventually withdrew the remark. The position in which the missionary finds himself is so often one in which the glory of God is assailed. If Gigen's mother recovers, the lamas will claim it as their cure. If she dies then the foreigner and his God will be the scapegoat. George now gave Gigen the remaining dosage for his mother and told him how to administer it. "Thank you! Thank you!" they all said in their strange tongue-sucking obsequious fashion. "Do not thank me," said George. "It is to God all your thanks must be given." It has been rather a stormy finish but all part of the inevitable conflict with the powers of darkness here. Our hearts yearn for them. After this I do not think we spoke again to any of the Lord Jesus Christ; not that we were unwilling or were offended but somehow a crisis had been reached, a challenge had been issued and the time had come for us to leave.

CHAPTER ELEVEN

THEY SHOT TO KILL

THE following morning we assembled at the gates of Gigen's courtyard with the entire household giving us a last look over. For some of them this would be the first contact they had ever had with Europeans. Ere we left, we took a few photos, then jumping on our horses galloped away across the ploughed fields. As we turned to give a final wave, I suddenly felt a sadness at the parting. There they stood, a little group of some twenty Tibetan folk who, apart from the working of the Holy Spirit through the Word delivered to them, will go on turning their prayer wheels, mumbling their liturgies, belabouring their drums, calling on their lamas, burning their incense, herding their cattle, handling their crops and eating their tsamba in their big dark rooms and windy tents until the day dawn for us and the eternal gloom for them.

Gigen himself did not accompany us, but one of Bay-Ma's men continued with our little caravan to guide us over the passes to Bay-Ma's home. On our first day out from the village we were stopped en route by travellers wanting medical treatment. One woman we saw had the most incredible wart-like growth on her face. No doubt it was some form of goitre, a condition very common in the high mountains where the water is so pure and iodine salts are lacking. Early in the afternoon, to our surprise a young lama came across the river and taking the halter of George's horse led us over to a couple of houses situated on the farther bank. Unbeknown to us it had been agreed that we were to stay the night here as the local lamas had connections with Gigen's old lamasery. It was quite a wealthy community with several resident priests. After a meal we began to see why these people had been so anxious for us to come to their house. We were taken into a shadowed corner of the room where, quite unnoticed, lay a girl aged between twenty and thirty. She was of a pallid appearance and looked so pathetic amongst the dirty bedclothes. The men of the house told us she had lain there eight years. Was there anything we could do? A medical examination revealed the cause of her condition. There was a large growth in her abdomen. She needed to be taken to Kangting for immediate surgery. We now went to the second house where we had a further session with various sick folk until we were finally brought back to be shown our sleeping quarters. We were given the best room in the house, and from the Tibetan point of view that is always the god-room. It was an extraordinary experience going to sleep under the sightless gaze of numerous idols. They were strange vigilants but, needless to say, did not molest us. Whilst staying in this place several of the lamas received Christian literature and with one we had a serious conversation on spiritual issues.

It took almost another three days to reach Bay-Ma's valley. The trail lay over tremendous country. In addition to fresh vistas of mighty ranges and snow-filled horizons we came across a very peculiar natural feature at great altitude. This was a huge crater. Whether it was volcanic in origin was difficult to say, but as we skirted it I estimated its diameter as four miles. Once we had negotiated the lip of this giant saucer we were obliged to descend through deep snow. We came down into an inhabited valley and passed through a village where, sad to say, we found hardly a man sober. This is unusual amongst the Tibetans but it was a day of festivities and the crude spirits had been too much for them.

As we approached Bay-Ma's country we met large crowds of Tibetans. They were dressed in their finest clothes, some of them looking very colourful with their gay hats, furs and tastefully designed top boots. We joined them in one of the big houses, but it was unpleasant indoors because myriads of flies were plaguing the district. There was also a good bit of carousing going on and we found our interest lay much more with the fierce horseriding convened in the open fields. The ironical thing about the races was that the start and finish were so undefined. I could never really tell who won, but then nobody seemed to care. They so enjoyed the ride! It was on the Monday afternoon, November 15th, that we eventually rode up to the Bay-Ma establishment. There were two houses and their adjoining compounds and a hundred yards or more away his nomad tent. We were warmly received by his wife Number One. As soon as we saw her we were aware that she was a woman who was his intellectual equal. It was in her hands that all his affairs were left while he taught in Kangting. His other wives were more the cattle girls and were, I should imagine, the equivalent of concubines. Wife Number One now showed us around the premises and Bay-Ma, who was very obviously in charge, shouted orders to his people and had them running around looking after our tents and equipment.

In a comparatively short while our camp was pitched alongside his and we had become integrated to his whole community.

There now followed several days of leisurely contact with these nomad folk. We were in and out of their houses and spent much time in the tents. The womenfolk dealt with the yak, grazed them and milked them and staked the calves inside the tent at night. Bay-Ma was very busy but never neglectful of his guests. He kept us plied with milk, butter, cheese and thick steaks of yak meat. Whilst we were there he was also preparing skins for clothing. It was interesting to see how he took a pelt and gradually worked it until it was soft and pliable. How self-supporting these people are! Their fields supply the barley for tsamba and their herds and flocks, their other staple foods. The hides, hooves and horns of the animals are all utilised. They make their own yak's hair rope, spin their wool on twirling little hand-spindles and then weave it into cloth on their primitive looms. Needlework is the man's job, the materials used being so coarse. It is staggering to think of this hardy race being shut off from the outside world so long and yet able to survive. Bay-Ma, it appeared, was also involved in some local 'election'. One day we noticed he was collecting together various gifts, amongst them two cuts of leather for a pair of boots and a sack of grain or peas. He also took out some documents which he wrapped carefully in a piece of cloth. We wondered what it was all about, but it became increasingly obvious that Bay-Ma was a man of influence and of growing power. In his own peculiar way he was a forceful character brooking no defiance and submitting to no dishonour. If he objected to a remark passed over the camp fire then he could sit in silence until his critic was shamed into speaking. He was very faithful to us, but being Tibetan to the backbone I should imagine he would be a terror to his enemies. Our tent now became a daily dispensary where teeth were pulled (without anaesthetic), eyes were bathed, sores dressed, even my own festering finger 'plotted', and when possible the Gospel preached. Bay-Ma's Number One wife came along one day and we began to talk. She was fascinated to hear how Jesus was born and how he was laid in the hay beside the cattle in the stable. This was the nomad way. Did they not bear their children with the little calves close by? She began to talk about her family. The little girl we saw was Bay-Ma's only daughter, Pi-Ta. She was a cheery eight-year-old who loved to lie long in the morning snuggling down in her sheepskin gown. If you looked at her hair you would not know she was a girl at all. I doubt whether it had once been combed in her life! Perhaps she was not old enough for that yet, or perhaps the hair was not long enough! Combing hair for the Tibetan woman is an onerous task. They are expected to twine it into one hundred and eight separate plaits, one for every book in the Buddhist canon! Many women find their own hair inadequate for this oppressive hairstyle but, nothing daunted, a little hair from a yak's tail, being as black as their own, makes up the deficit. Thus far Pi-Ta showed no interest in such matters. Her very simple duties were to care for the baby yak. "Pi-Ta," said Number One wife, "calls me 'mother', but she is not really my own child. She was born to Bay-Ma by one of the other wives." She spoke quite naturally about these things and as far as I could see there was no bitterness or jealousy between these women, each of whom shewed a genuine affection for Bay-Ma himself. They each had an established place in the household and their particular work to do. They were well provided for by their mutual husband, and on the roof of the world I suppose that means a very great deal. Amongst the many interesting nomad characters we met was a fine looking young fellow called Lozang Sherab. We saw him first at the horse-racing of the recent festivities. We now learned he was the brother of the man who had guided us over the passes. The local folk called him Loshay for short and after a talk with Bay-Ma it was agreed by all concerned that Loshay should enter our employment and travel with us to Lhasa.

We had now been at the encampment nearly a week and were beginning to feel we should make a move, but another day or two passed and it was not until the 25th that we at last pulled up our tent pegs and bade farewell. Bay-Ma came a short distance with us just to make sure that we got away in good order and said that he expected to follow down to Kangting in a few days' time. "Galay Peb-ro," he cried, "Please go slowly! Please go slowly!" To which we answered "Galay Shu-ro!" "Please rest slowly! Please rest slowly!" So slowly we went on our way. Following us along the trail came a number of boys, and we could not fathom why they continued with us after Bay-Ma had gone. Then they entered a house and quickly reappeared with one of them carrying something in his arms. It was a kitten which they insisted on presenting to us. Tibetan dress lends itself particularly to this kind of thing. The big fold formed by the girded

Tibetan gown constitutes what they call the 'rum'. In this space all around the waist the Tibetan puts bowls, bags, pipes, snuff and, if necessary, even kittens! Over the first pass there was a lot of snow and the yak were difficult to manage. The sky became very black as dusk fell and, taking shelter in a house, we were obliged to spend the night in a very smoky room. The snowfall, however, was not too excessive and another two days' travel over the mountains brought us without further delays into our base at Kangting . . .

Loshay from the start was a first class servant. He could neither read nor write but had eyes like a hawk and a mind as sharp as a needle. One of his first achievements was to learn to make foreign bread. In fact he was game for all kinds of duties except one. I found this out one day when a scavenging dog frequenting the courtyard showed signs of madness. We told Loshay to go to our neighbour Jah across the way and ask for a loan of a gun. He had no objection to this because he loved guns, but when I said, "Now take that dog outside the courtyard and shoot it!" he was horrified. If it had been a question of assaulting a Chinese policeman and grabbing his firearm he would have done it in a moment, if given the chance. He was always on the lookout for such hair-raising escapades as this, but to shoot a dog—that was something too dreadful to be countenanced! It was undoubtedly a question of his Buddhist background, but it was peculiar how human blood to Loshay was never quite so sacred! It took a lot of persuasion but at last his conscience was convinced and one shot put the poor creature out of its agony and the whole courtyard from danger. The waters of the millstream quickly removed all evidence of the 'crime', carrying the corpse down into the river. It was amazing what went into that river. Once when looking over a bridge we saw beneath the crystal-clear current the tiny body of a dead child.

As the days passed we wondered why Bay-Ma was delayed so long. Nearly three weeks went by and then a messenger came in saying he would be down within three days. There had apparently been much work to do. The district guns were being tested and sorted and a local leader had to be chosen. It seemed that Bay-Ma was a favourite for this position. Several days later Loshay, the carefree horseman and courageous fighter, came rushing into the living room of Number Eighteen, Radiant Light Street hardly able to keep back the tears. Something catastrophic must have happened, and it had. Another moment or two, and one of Bay-Ma's wives ran in, sat down at the table and sobbed her heart out. We had never seen the imperturbable Tibetans so overwrought. As they blurted out their words we were dumbfounded to hear that Bay-Ma had been shot and killed on his way into Kangting. It was almost unbelievable. It was only after we had called in Gigen, and after Loshay and the woman had quietened sufficiently to speak more coherently, that we began to grasp the story. It seems that the election of the district leader had been accompanied by 'fierce words', particularly when Bay-Ma's support increased. In addition to this someone in Minya was in great debt to Bay-Ma and Bay-Ma had decided to go to Kangting with certain documents implicating his debtor before the Chinese courts. Taking his second wife with him, who always accompanied him on his journeys, he thought to slip quickly and unnoticed through the hills and accomplish his purpose. In their haste they camped at nightfall, a full hours' walking distance beyond the last hamlet. As they retired, a shot rang out in the darkness, then another and another. Bay-Ma was wounded and fell below some bushes. "Where are you?" his wife shouted. He managed to reply but it only betrayed his position. Two further shots stabbed through the darkness and Bay-Ma lay dead, wallowing in his own blood in the frozen wilderness of that December night. His wife ran for her life, but once she was at a safe distance she waited a long while in the stillness. Then courageously she returned, found the body of Bay-Ma and, assuring herself that he was already dead, raced at top speed through the night back to the encampment. Once the news was broken to the family, wife Number Three set out for Kangting. It must have been a rugged breathless journey, and now here she was breaking her heart in the very house where her husband had taught me the language so faithfully.

As soon as it was known, thirty Tibetans rallied together and left Kangting for Bay-Ma's country. Whilst on the fringe of this wild area there were the Chinese courts, Tibetans had their own ways of securing justice. They are also great detectives. The relatives of Bay-Ma's first wife needed to be informed at all costs. This was a question of honour. From then on the feud would develop and they would not rest until vengeance had been taken and perhaps more than taken. In this way the tragedy is perpetuated for generations. Loshay gradually pieced together for us the different clues. The footprints in the snow revealed that there were two men involved in the murder, one tall and the other short. Bullet cases were found which pointed to the type of gun used. It so happened that because these particular bullets were peculiar to one type of gun, only two of which were known to exist in the area, a strong lead in the case was established. These clues, once fitted against the background of all the known enmities in Bay-Ma's life, issued in a murder hunt in the mountains which, as far as we heard, was not without result. The details of what followed were for the most part deliberately kept from our ears but I should imagine the men concerned wished they had never been born. Bay-Ma had been a great teacher and had so genuinely befriended us. I could not help but think of him. As he lay dying, I wondered—what were his closing thoughts? Could it be in the brief moment, ere he was hurtled into eternity, that he turned to the Christ of whom he had read so much in my little white-washed room?

CHAPTER TWELVE

THE WEAK GOD WINS

GUNKA was a tall genteel Tibetan, of softer disposition than most of his race, not as clever as Bay-Ma, nor as scholarly as Gigen and poles apart from young Loshay. He was not a lama although trained, I believe, in a lamasery as a young man. He was married and had one child. His home, like himself, was neatly kept. In fact he was an artist and this no doubt accounted for his unusual temperament. I saw some of his work and I must say it was brilliantly executed. This, then, was the man who now became my teacher. He sat where Bay-Ma used to sit and did the work that Bay-Ma used to do. Under his patient guidance and instruction I read the major part of Mark's Gospel in Tibetan.

One evening not long after Bay-Ma's tragic death we had another shock. Jah's servant came dashing in from across the road to tell us that his master had had a fearful accident. As we received the news, I knew that George's thoughts were the same as mine. Jah was in touch with the Lhasa Government on our behalf and was securing permission for us to enter Tibet. Could it be that Satan had struck him down? The shock of Bay-Ma's murder was still with us. Christ holds the keys of Death and of Hades but was not Satan at work somewhere in these incidents too? Leaving everything, we were over to Jah's place in a matter of moments. He lived in beautifully-furnished Tibetan apartments, had a large and handsome family and a wife who was a mother in a thousand. As we went in, the whole house was in a tumult. Mr. Jah, whilst hanging a picture, had fallen heavily, with the result that the broken glass had pierced his head. By the time we reached him he had already bled profusely. Someone in the house had had the presence of mind to clap a handful of tsamba flour over the wound and this had staunched the flow to some extent. With an antiseptic solution I began to wash the wound whilst George went across to the house for his surgical kit. It was a fearful gash right between the eye and the temple. A fraction of an inch either way, and he would either have lost his eye or, worse still, his life. The minutes ticked by and I wondered whenever George would return. I could see it was serious, but I did not realise how dangerous it was. George had done no stitching for two years and now he was obliged to give a local anaesthetic and stitch this wound in such a critical part of the head. With his limited experience he trembled to handle the situation but the wound needed immediate attention. So much seemed to be involved, not only the man's life but the whole future of the work itself. After deliberately taking time for prayer, George at last returned and set to work. Several days later when we took out the stitches we saw how God had answered. The wound was healthy and the skin knitting together very well. After his recovery Jah could not do enough for us. China's second currency in three years was skyrocketing to extinction and we were obliged to have bank accounts in different cities and deal in gold dust, silver dollars, tea and silk. With his extensive contacts in West China, Jah put us in touch with a merchant in

Chengtu. When we went down country to purchase supplies and contact the churches there, we visited this man and were amply repaid. We bought, on that occasion, nearly £150 worth of cloth to carry on trade in the interior when cut off from the outside world. On its arrival some weeks later in Kangting, such was the current market price that its value had already trebled. It was partly due to this capital that I was later on able to live hundreds of miles deep in the plateau, after George had gone through South-East Tibet to India. Truly the provisions of God are beyond all prediction.

Things in Kangting were now getting very explosive. From this high mountain town we were, in a sense, looking down on China in those last convulsions which led to the final overthrow of the Chiang Kai-shek régime by the forces of Communism. This meant the time was ripe for a local Tibetan uprising and when we sat at night upstairs in Number Eighteen, Radiant Light Street we would start uneasily every time there was the shot of a gun. The Tibetans were trigger-happy even in normal times, but now anything might happen. Loshay kept us in touch with the feelings of the rank and file and our contacts with Jah and Pangda Tsang* informed us of movements in high places. How much longer law and order could be maintained was open to question. This was evidenced when a Tibetan detained in the Chinese police station was forcibly released by a mob of his compatriots. The town was a political volcano and no one knew when the eruption would begin.

One night a shot rang out, followed by a patter of feet which did not stop running until they were outside

* i.e. 'the House of Pangda'.

our front door. A few words told us the worst. Someone had been shot just down the road. We were whisked off through the alleys to a Chinese dwelling, then upstairs into a cramped little room where we saw, to all intents and purposes, a dead man with his entire nose blown away and a blood-filled hole where his eye had been. A closer look revealed another wound on the side of his head. What had happened was hard to say. Someone said he had been cleaning a rifle but we had no time to argue. His heart was still beating, but we were powerless to do anything. There was only one course to be taken. We must get him to the Roman Catholic hospital, even if he die on the way. They at least, were surgically equipped to handle the case. Six burly Tibetans carried the blood-drenched man bodily all the way to their unit. As we escorted him in, we were received by two nuns, one a doctor and the other a nurse, and for the next three hours we were working together in their little operating theatre fighting for the man's life. The bullet had gone right through his head and out the other side but without tearing the brain tissue. A drip was rigged up and after certain necessary preparations, the stitching began. It took thirty-seven stitches to draw together the ragged pieces of skin that were once the nose. The eye was away and the cavity could only be closed up. The hole in the head was kept open to drain the wound. That he was still alive was a miracle of the grace of God. Though it may seem incredible, within three weeks the man was on his feet. Yet that is not the end of the story. A few weeks later still, he was shot again! Somebody in a doorway fired at him and wounded his thigh. Kangting in those days was a wild-west town!

In the midst of increasing tension we had two interesting respites. One was a hunting trip and the other a three days' feast at a place called Er Dao Chao outside Kangting. These two ventures marked a deeper intimacy with Pangda Dopgyay and his friends, a confidence out of which grew his suggestion that we should accompany him into the interior, some three hundred miles west, to his mountain retreat at Po. This was a small but strategic village not far from that almost legendary river, the River of Golden Sand. These two ventures had some breathtaking moments. On the hunting trip we were taken away up into the savage country above Kangting where blue goat and deer can be shot high on the ridges. It was fantastic to see the Tibetans bring down these animals to the base camp having shot them at immense distances and carried them over rock and fell, all at heights between 12,000 and 19,000 feet. Pangda Dopgyay would then call for warm blood drawn from the heart of the freshly-killed animal and as evening drew in we would sit around eating their boiled venison. We did not mind the meat but the blood, to put it mildly was not exactly our 'cup of tea'! The feast at Er Dao Chao was none the less hair-raising, although of a different nature. The Tibetans expected George and I to perform our 'native dances' or sing our 'native songs' for their entertainment. Then we went swimming with them (hardly one of whom could swim) in an ice-cold tarn. Whilst it provided ample amusement to the Tibetans it was rather an unexpected missionary duty! It ended up by my having to fish Pangda Dopgyay's son out of a deep pool where he would otherwise have drowned! The waters of Central Asia fed from eternal snows are, to my mind, not for swimming in; and if Tibetans, who for the most part live more than a thousand miles from the sea, would humbly accept that fact it would be easier for all concerned!

With such contacts as these, our Tibetan language was progressing by leaps and bounds. We were hearing and using it everyday and Gunka was beginning to enjoy his work because we could discuss things much more thoroughly now. Persevering day by day we now came to that part of the Gospel story where the events prior to the crucifixion mount to their climax. We read together of Peter and how he denied his Lord. Then we followed Jesus to Gethsemane and pondered his great agony. Gunka read for the first time in his life the great words 'If it be possible let this cup pass from me, nevertheless not what I will but what thou wilt'. Suddenly Gunka's face flushed beneath his sallow skin and putting his head in his hands he did what Tibetans never do, he began to cry. I sat perfectly still and earnestly prayed. Then quietly he rose from his stool and left the room.

Some of the great cities of China had now fallen to the Communists and the Tibetan leaders headed by Pangda Dopgyay were carefully judging their moment of departure for the interior. George and I were all set. Medicines and Scriptures had already been dispatched by yak-train into the hinterland. Animals were at the alert and we only awaited the word. Then, in an atmosphere of crisis, it came. What a morning as we assembled with the great caravan massing in Pangda Dopgyay's courtyard! There were scores of pack-animals and a host of following horsemen. Kangting had not seen such a day for half a century. The Chinese forces were powerless to restrain Dopgyay, with popular feeling running so high; but to let him go with all his potential power for organising a Tibetan uprising was galling indeed. In a wild flurry of prancing horses, jostling riders and scattered silver coins for the waiting paupers, the House of Pangda, in all the regalia of Tibetan aristocracy, marched triumphantly on its way into the mountain fastness of Tibet.

Outside on the rocky road beyond Kangting stood a lonely figure. As I approached him on my horse, I saw to my delight it was my teacher Gunka. Politely he came forward and as I dismounted he handed me the ceremonial white scarf of Tibetan custom. It was a touching and respectful farewell from this gracious Tibetan, whom I had come to esteem so much. We said our last 'Galay Peb-ro's' and final 'Galay Shu-ro's' and then headed into the Great Beyond. The sky was still grey but I was conscious of the sunshine breaking through.

Later I heard the wonderful news that Gunka, touched by the loving hand of God, had received the Christ of Calvary as His own personal Saviour. In love for his new-found Lord he returned to his home and destroyed his idols. The proud buddhas and ferocious gods of the temple could hold him no more. He had come to Jesus.

> 'The other gods were strong but Thou wast weak;
> They rode, but Thou didst stumble to a throne
> But to our wounds God's wounds alone can speak
> And not a god has wounds, but Thou alone.'*

* Edward Shillito, 1872-1948.

Strange to say, Gunka's witness was only for a little while. Not long after his conversion he died of tuberculosis and passed into the presence of God. In the face of things so inscrutable the answer of the Word alone suffices. 'Precious in the sight of the Lord is the death of His saints.'

CHAPTER THIRTEEN

INTO THE GREAT BEYOND

FAR away behind the ranges, where the frontiers of China and Tibet merge in an unexplored wilderness of mountains, there stands in a secluded valley the great white house of Pangda Tsang. The changing fortunes of his family in the hierarchy of the Lhasa government had compelled him, in years gone by, to retire to this sequestered spot. He had fought, admittedly, against the central Tibetan authority, yet it had not been for personal ambition but for a new Tibet. When this revolution failed he could only flee to the frontier regions and await his time. One day his country would need him. He would be ready then. In the hidden valley of Po he sought to produce in miniature the state of which he dreamed. He developed the land, turning the open pasture into fruitful ground. He built his great feudal fortress and established law through all the bandit-ridden mountains till not a man would lift a finger against anything, or anyone, called Pangda Tsang's. Those soldiers who were loyal to him became the basis of this new community. Each man received a plot on which to grow his barley and little houses began to rise. Some longed for battle in the hills but Pangda Dopgyay had seen too many warriors lie dying in the snow. The years slipped by and Po became established, but his great desire for an independent and prosperous Tibet still burned. In order to explore every possibility he moved with his family to Kangting. Wealth and prestige steadily increased. He and his brother Pangda Rapga visited Nanking. They wanted a mandate for the Tibetan people from the Chiang Kai-shek régime. Much was discussed; even more was promised but nothing was effected . . . So he returns to Kangting and Rapga joins him. Meanwhile all the sky of China reddens with Communism and all its earth with blood. The corrupted rule of Chiang Kai-shek totters and falls to ruin. Perhaps this is the time, the time of all the years, for the House of Pangda. Can it be that, reunited with Lhasa, they can hold the Chinese hordes on the high battlements of the plateau until the world at large has recognised Tibet once more as a sovereign state? It was at such a time we were asked to travel with him to his distant mountain retreat. As the negotiations with Lhasa through Jah, our neighbour, began to falter, this unexpected door swung open. We saw it as an iron gate yielding and thus went through it under the hand of God . . .

There in that distant valley excitement stirs. The great white house, empty and silent through the years, bustles with excitement once again. It is all the talk in the village, and the little children who have never seen the lord of the valley hear with awe and animation that their master must soon return. Down in the stables the famous white war-horse, now twenty years old, still munches quietly at the hay. No one has ridden him since Pangda Dopgyay went away; and out in the wide courtyards the hunting dogs roam aimlessly, waiting for a gun to point them to the hills . . .

Behind us the multitudes dwindle. The clamour of voices fades to a whisper. The mountains rise, and the trail winds outward into the great silence. All one hears is the metallic strike of the horses' hooves upon the rock-strewn way. The heaving warmth of the animal slowly creeps through the legs and one thrills again to the sight of the road which leads us on into the vast unknown of Central Asia. Through all that matchless country we move, under a cloudless sky by day and a star-filled heaven by night. The long caravan ambles its way through the defiles and over the passes; it meanders by distant hamlets and traverses barren grasslands dotted with nomad tents. We cross the mighty waters of Nya Chuka, where two large tributaries of the Yangtze converge beneath the sinister shadows of towering crags. We enter still wilder country and Pangda Dopgyay's retainers fan out to rout the bandits lurking in the hollows. As darkness falls, men open fire from the cliffs above. It is immediately returned from rifles in the camp. Perhaps it was a test of strength or just a robbers' welcome. Yet who can tell? The firing ceases and the night reverts to its coolness and its calm. Vast areas of the plateau are both treeless and manless. Earlier in the year it would have been green and inviting but now the broad vales are parched and cheerless. The icy wind soughs through the dry giant sorrel. Above our heads the hawks circle endlessly and vultures tear out the entrails of any hapless mule that falters on the track. The higher we go, the smaller the streams become, until they are mere trickles gurgling over the cold grey stones. Yet even here the minnows dart through the pools and tiny birds skim across the boulders. Most flowers have already perished but nodding edelweiss, such hardy mountain folk, still turn their faded faces sunwards, gazing from the frozen void into the icy dome above. Then where the yak trails, marked by the endless hoof-worn ruts, stretch out across the undulating lands, all the way is strewn with cattle-dung and bones bleached white in the sun. Here and there a tuft of marshy grass will raise its hostile spines and some small bush burst into a flame of autumn red. At intervals three blackened stones tell of a traveller's fire and a camp of yesternight pitched in the dusk . . . So does the eye reach out to the far horizons until the heart and mind bow with emotional exhaustion at the immanence of God . . . There in the far distance I see the trail bite deep into the bare shoulder of the hill, its plurality of paths like furrows laid upon a human back. My vision follows it upward to the place where sky and ridges meet. We shall be there tomorrow . . . and so will every man. It is our great necessity; the climax of the pilgrimage of life. Our path across this barren earth must needs, at last, run out over the hill. Yet heaven and earth have met in Jesus, and through His Calvary-road all God's mountains have become a way . . .

On November 1st we arrived at Litang. We were now sixteen days out from Kangting and seven days distant from Po. The place where we were accommodated was the house in which the sixth Dalai Lama was born. This fact was publicised by a strange wooden object, something like a dumb-bell, hanging outside the gate; a sullen, yet thought-provoking memorial . . .

. . . My mind goes back through the centuries and I see the official party of riders dropping down from the high trails to the west. They are approaching this distant city of Litang, scanning all the environs for any special feature indicated by the state oracle of the

Lhasa government. They have been searching for years but thus far in vain. They feel it is time for the deceased fifth Dalai Lama to be returning to earth once more. Then they espy this house where we are staying. It lies below the twin cities of this renowned centre of Lamaism. Is it the flash of gold from the lamasery pinnacle that catches their eye? Is it a distant clump of trees, or the dark sky-line of the mountains? It can be one of many things but whatever it is, it is enough to kindle their hopes that this is the place where the sixth Dalai Lama will be found. In view of the propitious signs they withdraw to some secluded spot and there the officials exchange their clothes for the humble attire of their servants and in this disguise go now to the house of their expectations. In an informal way they contact the resident families, taking every opportunity to observe the male children of about five years of age and under. Unobtrusively they bring these boys into close proximity with articles worn or used by the fifth Dalai Lama in his lifetime. They carefully scrutinise their attitudes and responses, watching hopefully for any flash of recognition, for should not the fifth Dalai Lama in his sixth 'incarnation' recognise what is essentially his own? From these early advances they form their preliminary judgements. In all this they are careful to arouse no suspicion, but returning to their hide-out, dress themselves once more in their official robes. A short time is allowed to elapse and then they ride up to the house to conduct their official examination of the boys they feel most likely to provide the looked-for successor. Now from the numerous articles one boy chooses the very articles used by the erstwhile fifth Dalai Lama, and these in preference to any others.

The officials confer and are unanimous that their quest has ended. The indications of the state oracle concerning location, setting and appearance of the birth place are all authenticated. A child in this very place has correctly responded. The result is that Lhasa is immediately notified and arrangements are made to transport the boy and his parents to the capital. For them life will never be normal again. Soon the official acknowledgement of the incarnation is proclaimed by the Lhasa government. At this the boy is immediately deified. Men fall down and worship him. He is segregated from all except his tutors and servants, and in the isolation of his imagined godhood he becomes the centre of the theocratic rule of the whole land of Tibet . . . This is the fantasy and living blasphemy into which the boy is propelled by the lamaistic authorities. This occult practice has proceeded along these lines for centuries as the means of identifying the successor to the Dalai Lama's religious and political throne. As we lived in the old house in Litang and strolled about its barn-like interior, there was only the wooden 'dumb-bell' at the door to remind us that these very walls had witnessed such an astonishing ceremony as this.

Litang itself is divided into two parts. There is the city of the laity and the city of the priesthood. The former is comprised of one long dusty street bordered by flat-roofed one-storey dwellings. At the time we were there, part of the built-up area was in ruins owing to earthquakes. Between our lodging place and the town was a big open green where day after day hundreds of yak were slaughtered. Every fifty yards or so, across this open stretch of grass, a group of Tibetans was camping out. There they were, living amidst piles of reeking yak skins, and all around them the blood-soaked earth. Hung up on wooden stands were sides of yak flesh waiting to be bought. These were mostly purchased by the lamasery which, though it condemned the killing of animals, was content to dry the meat over the cold winter months and then eat it, or even sell it the following spring. Scavenger dogs prowled to and fro cringing before stones and curses as they sought for scraps of flesh, whilst audacious crows swooped down from the skies hoping also to take their fill.

During our eleven-day stay in the town which is, I believe, at 14,500 feet the second-highest in the world, we met a Chinese lama. As I talked with him I found he was a graduate of Dairien University.* He offered to escort me around the great lama-city. Litang lamasery is the fourth-largest of its kind, and has attached to it, although not always in residence, something like four thousand monks. Passing out of the civil city we crossed a narrow lane and entered into the religious city. To our left and right were the houses of the lamas, white buildings with ornate windows and sometimes slanting roofs. They stood together in clumps, the spaces between them making irregular and often narrow streets running off the main roadway. At the rear of the city new buildings were being erected. After hundreds of years Lamaism was still growing and fabulous sums of money were being raised to extend these halls of Satan. Almost every square inch of the interiors was being prepared for the overlaying of gold and costly paint-work. Eventually my guide brought me to the main temple at the heart of the lama citadel. Although a

* In N.E. China.

stranger I was nevertheless permitted to walk in. The floor was panelled in polished wood. The lofty ceiling was supported by carved red pillars inlaid with gold. On the east, west and south sides of the hall were balconies which overlooked a large area used as an auditorium for large priestly assemblies. The whole architecture of the building concentrated one's attention on the north side where two wrought-iron gates, some twenty feet high and twelve feet broad, guarded a black, foreboding enclosure. We crossed the smooth wooden floor where little sparrows hopped merrily about, and peered through the steely trellis of those imposing gates. The region beyond was so dark that at first nothing was discernible. Then gradually I was conscious of a few temple lamps burning dimly somewhere above us. As I peered upwards beyond the lamps I saw at a height of some forty feet a gigantic gilt face gazing blankly and serenely into space. The pale glimmer of burning butter was the only illumination; the impression of other-worldliness complete. In sheer astonishment, and perhaps a little unnerved, I turned to the young Chinese lama and asked him intently, "Do you worship that?" Without a flicker of embarrassment he unequivocally replied, "I do! That is Buddha". Outside we talked together for a long time, and I poured the Gospel into his ear until he knew, even if he did not acknowledge it, that the light of the knowledge of the glory of God shines from one face alone—the face of Jesus Christ.

CHAPTER FOURTEEN

THE HIDDEN VALLEY

THE day we left Litang, Loshay had a sore head. It was one thing to lose Dom-Nag, or even a silver bowl, but to lose Loshay would have been a tragedy. Yet in a bloodthirsty brawl he had come as near to getting murdered as he would ever want to be in his life. What disturbed us was that he had fought for 'our interests'! Someone we had entertained, apparently, had stolen a silver bowl—at least that was Loshay's theory—and of course, until he retrieved it he felt his name was hardly clear, so off he went and, being the sleuth that he was, narrowed down his man. He sat down beside him somewhere up in Litang and promptly began to feel for the stolen bowl in the fold of his gown but the man was not having any and drew his sword. A fight to the death ensued in which Loshay almost had his skull broken, and the other man ended up with a yak's horn through his forehead. As a Tibetan would sooner lose his head than his honour, Loshay continued with us, sore but not sorry. And what more could we say! Although Dom-Nag seemed also to have disappeared somewhere, the livestock side of our personal entourage was now enhanced by 'the grey'. This was a magnificent fiery animal, a terror at first, but later to prove a fast, efficient steed, especially for shorter distances. Pangda Dopgyay arranged the purchase from a lama who was scared stiff of the creature, and George had the nerve-racking task of bringing it under control. How he was not mangled beneath its plunging hooves was something of a miracle but he eventually emerged as its master. In one of its more uncontrollable moments he collided with the weighty centurion of Pangda's army and bounced him clean out of his saddle on to the ground—an indignity which he took with surprising good humour.

The whole caravan, now more than two hundred animals strong, took two hours to cross the Litang plain. At about 17,000 feet we pitched camp in the shelter of a great boulder. I felt particularly bad-tempered as we struggled to put up the tent but George, a little more gracious than his 'Scots temperament' would normally allow, kindly suggested it was the altitude! Around the camp the yak grew restive and with so many of them about it looked as if the tent would be ripped to pieces before the dawn. The following day we climbed still higher. Huge pyramid-shapes of rock soared above us and we came to a lovely lake which for some unaccountable reason was not completely frozen over. On reaching the top of the pass, at what must have been almost 18,000 feet, the most entrancing spectacle lay before us. The snow range on our immediate horizon, according to the National Geographical Society records, rose to 22,000 feet. One of its most outstanding peaks was very similar to the Matterhorn. We descended for hours through sand, dust and rock until we reached the grassy floor of the valley 3,000 or 4,000 feet below. From now on, at intervals all along the way, groups of Tibetans gathered to welcome the Pangda brothers back to their old estate. They came, some of them on horseback and in great finery; others, like the humble nomad women, bringing bowls of milk for them to touch, even if they could not stop to drink. In some areas the population was surprising. From what seemed a vacant world, people emerged from the folds of the grasslands, like so many moles coming out of their burrows. More and more riders joined the party until, as the days passed, we became a veritable company of cavalry advancing on Tibet! To see a band of fully-armed Kambas* suddenly swirl round a knoll of the hills was enough to make your blood run cold, but all proved to be friends and every contingent bent on welcome. We were now in territory with a hundred per cent Tibetan population, Even our party could muster only one Chinese. He was Pangda Dopgyay's secretary. I do not think this gentleman in the long blue gown had ever ridden before and as we journeyed over hill and dale he went through agonies. Clinging pitifully to his saddle fore and aft, he could be heard muttering most pitifully, "Ai Ya! Ai Ya!" at every lurch of his mule. This rhymic lamentation was too much for the teenage sons of Dopgyay and Rapga. With a mischievous crack of his whip, Jigme came behind the mule and gave it a sharp flick across its buttocks. The result was almost catastrophic for the pathetic Chinese secretary. In reality, however, he *was* pathetic, for he had long succumbed to opium and I genuinely believe it was more for compassionate reasons than anything else that Dopgyay had brought him along.

After nearly a week's riding out of Litang, we topped the final pass that marked the beginning of the long descent to Po. The scene was mighty. Below us there

* The type of Tibetans inhabiting the Sikang province.

dropped away a vast belt of pinewoods through which the rough track steeply zig-zagged down. Across the yawning valley, buttresses of rock rose sheer, thousands of feet above the forest. In lofty crevices snow had accumulated, whilst at lower levels the shale screes splayed their rubble fingers through the trees. Far, far below stood the big white house and the diminutive dwellings of the villagers. One of the riders assured me this was Po, and I knew that in an hour or two we would be at journey's end. Down and down we went, the rocky, dusty path winding through the great firs. Now and then we passed through an area of dead trees and the brilliant sunshine streamed in slanting rays through the ghostly branches, to illuminate the gloom. Just a few moments and we would be plunged into shadow yet again. It was fascinating tracing the figures of the men walking their horses, twisting this way and that round the boulders and the fallen trees. In the heart of the pine forest, and still well above the village, Pangda Dopgyay was met by local womenfolk with more milk for him to drink. The descent seemed endless, but then the firs gradually yielded to a kind of holly and the vegetation softened. At long last we burst out into the sunshine and the riders filed one by one along the narrow path to the village, all agog with expectation. As we came to the first open fields large numbers of children came scampering towards us, thrilled at the gay sight of the horsemen and the never-ending caravan emerging from the forest. The white house loomed large before us and the road up to it was black with people. I was right behind Dopgyay as we came into the final straight. Two men waited in the crowded pathway, old associates of Dopgyay in those first days of the Po settlement. One readily acknowledged him, but the other in all the excitement failed to recognise him after the years. Realising his mistake the poor man cried aloud but Dopgyay, ignoring his emotion, handed him his bridle and gave him the honour of leading him in. Down through the village came the whole cavalcade, and then clattering up over the little wooden bridge, we flooded into the courtyards, filling them to overflowing. From the eaves of the white house fluttered fresh prayer flags, and lucky Tibetan signs were much in evidence. The escorting horsemen brought the Pangda brothers to the main door of the big fortress. This was their looked-for moment of achievement. They had brought their master home; and with their mission fulfilled they wheeled their horses sharply and dispersed into the countryside . . .

Now we see the Pangda Tsangs as any other family. Into the house they storm. Every room has to be explored. Every door opened. If it is locked, then it is rattled impatiently until the steward brings the keys. First we go to the main living room right up on the third floor. Much cleaning has been done but the pictures on the wall are soiled with the years and Jigme exclaims, "Why, these were all new when we left!" Then on to the flat roof, from where we survey the cultivated fields and the homes of the people. Then down again through the other apartments. "This room is for Rabga and his wife," says Dopgyay. He passes quickly on, "And this is our room," he tells us. We learn that the whole house is planned to withstand fire. Every detail, he assures us, was his personal design. We look in wonder at the solid beams and the high ceilings of the large rooms. We see the roof-top dancing-court, and scan the big medieval kitchen, finally descending to the ground floor and its ample store rooms. We are amazed at the whole gigantic structure erected with man's bare hands and the primitive tools of the Tibetan hinterland. After a first meal together in the big white house we go out into the main courtyard and are surprised to see a full-grown deer with antlers. It had been reared from a tiny fawn and kept as a pet. "But where is the famous white horse?" somebody asks. In a moment or two it is led into the yard. It is massive still. Pangda Dopgyay strokes its tail but as might be expected there is no flicker of recognition. The hunting dogs follow at our heels and seem to sense the excitement in the air. "And where is the big stone that only one man in the valley can lift?" "Out there in front of the house!" somebody answers. We all gather around the stone and one after another of Dopgyay's men try their strength. But they are weak after life in the town. At last we are led over to the place where, for the time being, we are to make our home. It is a little log cabin with a fireplace in the middle of the floor. Loshay tethers 'the grey', carries our bedding in, and dumps it on the two simple beds made of boards placed across some logs. We spread out our saddle-rugs, get a fire going, and settle in. It is one of those moments when thankfulness ceases to be just a verbal expression. Like a spring, it was rising in our hearts.

CHAPTER FIFTEEN

THE LONE ASSIGNMENT

THE shapely arms of the valley draped with fir stretched out and upwards to embrace the greying sky and, far above, the jagged fingers of the heights were already clasping at the mist and clouds. Away to the south I could see a distant trail slashed up through the forest till it broke across a grassy ridge to the west and beyond . . . I stood watching the figure of my fellow-labourer move slowly on toward the lonely pass. The sound of the horses' hooves grew fainter until it was lost in the ravine . . . Beyond the mighty passes to the west flowed the River of Golden Sand and beyond the 'big river' the foreboding territory of Lhasa-controlled Tibet. I turned at last, strangely alone in all that uttermost country. My nearest European neighbour would now be some twenty-one days eastward through the high bandit country of Sikang and my only companions the Tibetan people to whom my God had sent me. Yet we believed that one must go and one must stay if we were to attack this Satanic stronghold and by the power of God see Christ enthroned in ruined souls as yet still cringing in the shadows of the Potala . . .

Now it was evening time and as I gazed wistfully from the window of the little log cabin I instinctively looked again, in that great direction. The long shadows of the night were reaching out from the western ridges and creeping stealthily over the hamlet in the hollow. Above the low mud houses of the village a group of woodcutters paused in the dusk to rest from their heavy loads. Womenfolk they were, with dishevelled hair, and proud, weatherbeaten faces singing out their broken songs to the evening sky. The sun dipped deeper till the trees on the eastern slopes merged in the twilight and one by one the golden crags above yielded their splendour to the night. I turned and looked with blurred eyes at the objects in the room. It was not easy to be alone . . . But this I knew—the cross was focussed now . . .

Then in they came, rough rollicking company crowding together in the confined space of the log cabin and crouching round the embers of the fire. I put on the gramophone and they sat spellbound, puffing their long pipes, making their candid comments, and drinking in the music and its song. It was a way through into the confidence of their race; a way into the secrets and yearnings of their hearts. And as I saw them there with their wild, tousled hair, clad in their greasy sheepskin gowns; as their strong defiant faces lit up in the firelight and I glimpsed the sparkling eyes of their dirty but rosy-cheeked children in the light of the butter lamp, my heart was drawn afresh to them in the love of God. And sometimes, as the rich bass voice of a Gospel singer rang out in such a setting, my whole being rose in answer to the great refrain . . .

'I'd rather have Jesus than silver or gold
I'd rather have Jesus than riches untold
I'd rather have Jesus than houses or lands,
I'd rather be led by His nail-pierced hands

Than to be the king of a vast domain
And be held in sins dread sway
I'd rather have Jesus than anything
This world affords to-day.'

The sequel to this story is
to be found in
the book
When Iron Gates Yield